.dannii
minogue
the biography

dannii minogue
the biography

Chas Newkey-Burden

JOHN BLAKE

Published by John Blake Publishing Ltd,
3 Bramber Court, 2 Bramber Road,
London W14 9PB, England

www.johnblakepublishing.co.uk

First published in paperback in 2010

ISBN: 978 1 84454 959 7

British Library Cataloguing-in-Publication Data:

A catalogue record for this book is available from the British Library.

Design by www.envydesign.co.uk

Printed in Great Britain by CPI Bookmarque Ltd, Croydon, CR0 4TD

3 5 7 9 10 8 6 4 2

Papers used by John Blake Publishing are natural, recyclable products
made from wood grown in sustainable forests. The manufacturing processes
conform to the environmental regulations of the country of origin.

contents

introduction

At the outset, the reader is invited to spare a thought for the less lucky Minogue girl who, as she was growing up and grappling with the identity issues life throws at us all in our younger years, was also becoming known in the public sphere – but only ever in reference to her more famous and more successful sister. Times must have been testing for her living in this sibling shadow. However, the *less* famous sibling in those days was not Dannii but *Kylie*. Prior to Kylie's signing up for the soap opera *Neighbours* in the mid-1980s, she was trailing in the wake of Dannii, who was one of Australia's biggest celebrities. Of course, since then, Kylie has become the more famous of the two sisters and indeed one of the most famous women on the planet. So, although it was Dannii who tasted fame first and then effectively launched both of their careers, nobody could sensibly deny that Kylie is now the bigger star of the Minogue sisters.

But Dannii's story is often far more eventful and inspiring. Naturally, she has forever been asked about how she feels about her sister's superior success. It is often lazily assumed that she has become famous only off the back of her sister's success and also sometimes taken for granted that she must therefore furiously resent Kylie.

Neither assumption is true, although Dannii does tire of the almost inevitable comparisons that are made between them during press interviews. Memo to the world: tread carefully if you want to head down that line of questioning, as you might just bite off more than you can chew.

'You make it sound like we're Siamese twins, some freak circus act,' Dannii once snapped. The reporter on the receiving end of this outburst recalls how her interviewee's demeanour changed radically as she made it. She remembers how angry and icy the Aussie became in an instant. As we shall see, Dannii is well equipped to hold her own in interviews with the newspapers, on radio and even on television, where she once threw water over her interviewer. On other days, though, Dannii has proven to be far more light-hearted about the comparison. In 1990, while preparing for a photoshoot for an Australian newspaper, her wardrobe assistant touched on this territory – and lived to tell the tale without a ticking-off from Dannii. 'Gosh,' said the assistant. 'You look so much like your sister when you put wigs on.'

Far from exploding, Dannii let out a childlike shriek of delight, and started singing a familiar song: 'I should be so lucky – lucky, lucky, lucky …'

But the younger Minogue sister deserves to be considered in her own right. So who is Dannii Minogue? She has worn so many different career hats – singing, acting, modelling, designing, presenting and judging – that she steadfastly resists professional pigeon-holing. What can be stated emphatically, though, is that for Dannii her career is of such importance to her that her life 'away from work' has been an elusive thing to find. There are few more focused celebrities in the modern age. She has been described as an 'ice queen' by several people. One of the people I interviewed for this book described how Dannii at first stands off from people until she has weighed them up. She is focused and ambitious, as evidenced throughout her life story. Indeed, we need look no further than her successful working relationship with Simon Cowell. The music and television guru has made no secret of his own ambition and competitiveness, nor his admiration for those who share it. He often speaks admiringly of the drive in the eyes of pop legend Beyoncé, and during an intimate interview with Piers Morgan he praised the celebrity journalist for his highly competitive nature.

How much of an impact Dannii's steely focus has had on her life generally will become apparent as her story unfolds in the pages ahead. By her own admission, she does not find it easy to put her career ambitions to one side and relax. 'I don't reflect or meditate, I'm thinking what I am going to do tomorrow. I find it very hard to switch off, my career is so important to me,' she said. She has always had a mixed relationship with fame and speaks of her experiences with memorable vividness. More than anything, she sees it as a gamble. 'It's like standing on the top of the Empire State Building in the wind and thinking, Hell! I'm going to fall off,' she once said. Another time she added, 'It's like twirling the gun barrel and not knowing where the bullet is.' Again she gave a sense of freefall when she said of her line of work, 'It's a roller-coaster ride – and you don't know who's operating the ride or if they'll send you off the rails.'

Dannii is an Australian who loves living in England, and she is also rather fond of America. Because of this, her approach to work conjures up extra challenges for her. 'The hardest thing is that you can never call in sick,' she said. 'It's not like they can send someone else in your place.' She paused, and added, 'I find jetlag the hardest thing for me. Some of my friends don't suffer at all, but travelling from London to Australia I feel like I've been turned upside down.'

You wouldn't think so, looking at her ever-fresh-looking face.

Wherever she is at any given time, the one thing Dannii insists on is being informed. She always wants to know what is going on and what is planned for her. 'The most important thing is to know what's happening around you,' she said. 'You have to delegate but knowing the business side is so important, as is having a business manager like mine.'

Of course, something she cannot influence is how obsessed the world is with her sister. In contrast to the earliest years of her career, when commentators speak of her now, they often do so in one predictable way: as the younger sister of global superstar Kylie Minogue. The rumours of intense competition between the sisters are rife. 'With Kylie, there's no sibling rivalry,' Dannii has insisted often. 'We're interested in each other's career, but when we're together show business is the last thing we talk about. We go on about the same sort of things as everyone else: relationships, gossip, clothes, feelings. We're not only sisters, but friends.' She added, 'People are always asking me if I'm following Kylie doing this, or Kylie doing that. You might as well try to compare me with any other f***ing pop star from the whole of history.'

That said, as she has conceded, many artists suffer from comparisons with someone else. Britney Spears and Christina Aguilera immediately spring to mind.

With an eventful love life and a number of controversial moments under her belt, Dannii has run the gamut of press coverage from the horribly hostile to the overwhelmingly positive. She does her best to shrug off the bad coverage. 'When you read that your sister is an alien and some paper has proved it by studying her ears, you realise you can't take things too seriously,' she said.

Dannii has thicker skin than many might realise, and is also a very straight-talker. 'She's very ambitious and she knows what she wants,' according to X Factor contestant Luke Bayer, who was in her category on the show. 'She's also very direct and honest. Like Simon Cowell, she will speak to you honestly, which is an excellent thing to have.'

Dannii herself agrees that she tells it like it is. 'I'm very honest,' she said. 'Everything is straight down the line with me, which is good but can prove hurtful to others. I say what I think without always fully considering the effect on other people. In my defence, I'd say that I far prefer people to be totally honest, even if I don't like what they say. There's a lot of sycophancy in the music business and I can't be doing with that.' Indeed, she is even honest about herself. 'I was the most crap singer and crap dancer and crap everything,' she once admitted, 'but I worked my bollocks off, because that's what I wanted to do.'

It is perhaps in part her tireless honesty that has won her such a huge gay following. Of course, her sister Kylie is absolute royalty in the gay-icon stakes, but Dannii too has built up a formidable body of gay admirers, as she is often reminded. 'At a party I was approached by a gay guy, who said, "I just want to tell you how much I love your work," ' she recalled. '[He said] "We can relate to you. You do what you want. Having to come out as a gay you have to have that confidence and on that level we really relate to you." '

Asked for her own explanation for her gay following, she added, 'I guess they admire an underdog, too.'

It is unclear exactly how she would fit into the role of an underdog. With a famous sister at her side and a comfortable childhood in her background, her story does not instantly scream 'underdog'. Perhaps, though, she is hinting that her position as the less famous Minogue sister gives her an underdog status. Still, with regular slots at gay festivals and nightclubs throughout her career, she is clearly doing something to keep the pink pounds flowing into her coffers.

She inspires women, too, with her stylish ways, as she frequently reinvents her look. Indeed, even within the space of one given year, she has often changed her hair length, colour and style dramatically. Many observers enjoy every minute of it and are both thrilled and inspired by her fashion style. Others are not so impressed. 'Some people,' she said witheringly, 'usually female journalists, interpret it as though you must be mentally unstable or terribly dissatisfied with your life and your looks if you're always trying to change them. They can't believe you can be happy with the way you are. But it's fun, it's just part of being a girl; it's like being allowed to use makeup. It's just getting in touch with my feminine side.'

She is also a compulsive shopper, particularly for new clothes. As we shall see, her spendthrift side at one point led her deep into financial trouble and to the brink of fiscal disaster, which led to her stripping off for *Playboy* magazine.

Her bestselling calendars have often been revealing raunchy affairs, too. No wonder they are snapped up so eagerly.

But Dannii has never been a prude. She has admitted that she sometimes checks into hotels using her 'porn name' – Pussy Jones – and also confesses to enjoying outdoor sex romps. 'It's my porn name – you know, the name of your first pet and your mother's maiden name,' she said. 'I've been checking in as "Miss P Jones" for a few years now, so I definitely need to think of a new one.'

Of course, Kylie's 'porn name' would be the same as Dannii's, she was reminded. 'No – I got in there first,' replied the ever-competitive Dannii. 'Anyway, she has loads of names she uses. I can't say what they are, though.'

Dannii's ambitions are widespread and eclectic. She has even donned a huge yellow plastic beak to appear in an advertisement for Penguin biscuits – not a career high point, to be fair. But she is self-assured. She has *had* to be to keep her place in the public eye over the past four decades. 'It's not about being cocky, it's about being proud of the talent you have,' she said. It is a nagging fear of obscurity – together with a strong sense of the fickle ways of fame – that keeps her going. 'There are always people waiting in the wings and that is constantly in the back of my mind,' she said some years ago of her quest for success and fame. 'I've got to work damn hard at this.' Not even her biggest critics could sensibly suggest that she has worked anything less than damn hard. As a person she had been perceived as hard, too. This has some truth to it, but there is, as we shall see throughout the story, another side to her. 'I know what people think about me – they think I'm tough, hard as nails,' she said. 'Well, I've had to survive in a ruthless business. But in private, ask any of my friends, I'm just a softie.'

Indeed, Dannii is celebrated by those nearest to her as a caring, maternal woman who will be generous and punctual with flowers and other presents for friends' special occasions. And, of course, when her sister battled cancer Dannii was wonderfully supportive.

Her fame has already spanned four decades and she is now as popular as ever. She also looks better than she ever has, and seems to have finally found the lasting romantic happiness that for so long eluded her. For so long she has fascinated the world, but who is the *real* Dannii Minogue?

Here is her story …

CHAPTER 1

the tomboy

'I'm from convict stock,' said Dannii Minogue in 2007, but she was only joking. In fact, she comes from a wonderful, loving and close family. 'I had such an incredible upbringing: I have two parents who formed a family around me,' she said while in more serious mood.

Indeed, she does, and the Minogues formed themselves into a comfortable and happy unit, which remains close to this day. Those who have observed a Celtic tint to her beautiful looks will not be entirely surprised by her heritage. Her mother was a ballet dancer called Carol who lived in the small South Wales town of Maesteg, near Swansea. Carol's family were good pillar-of-the-community folk who ran the local post office. They knew and were known by most people in the area. They lived in Wales until Carol was 12, when the family emigrated to Australia. Her parents,

Dennis and Millie, had decided after some discussion to move the family to Townsville in Queensland, which was not a simple or common move at the time. Prior to the middle of the 1940s, it was quite unusual for a family to uproot themselves from Wales and emigrate to the other side of the world. But, then, an 'assisted-passage scheme' was created and an estimated 710,000 Brits were tempted by the promise of a voyage 'Down Under' for just £10, becoming known as the '£10 Poms'. If ambition can run in the blood, then plenty was to be flowing through Carol's veins as a result of this trip, and it would be passed down again to both Dannii and Kylie. Carol's looks would actually be seen more in Kylie. Carol was and is a beautiful woman, like both of her daughters, but in size and facial character Kylie is definitely more similar to her.

The family set sail on the SS *New Australia* in April 1955. The parents were brimming with optimism and excitement, yet naturally there was a sense of trepidation too. Some of the information about this voyage came as a result of research that was recently undertaken personally by Dannii and Kylie. And, although Dannii's quip about 'convict stock' was merely a nod towards the 'convict Aussies' stereotype, it was not without some truth, for the sisters also discovered that their maternal great-grandfather was once imprisoned in HM Prison Gloucester, according to an 1891 census, although there is no record of what the man, Morgan Riddiford, was convicted of. Interestingly, a census from a decade later revealed that Aussie actor and sometime Kylie co-star Jason Donovan's great-grandfather also served time in a British jail. Robert Rowatt spent time in HM Prison Holloway, before it became the all-women's prison that it is today.

When the '£10 Poms' arrived in Australia, the family were six strong and, once they were there, two more sons were added to the healthy fold. They lived first in Melbourne and then moved north to Townsville. Carol was a shy teenager but she found the confidence to take part in dance competitions at the Townsville Theatre Royal. Her daughters would later take part in talent contests and, in Dannii's case, would graduate to become judges. She was often triumphant in these contests, just as her two daughters would later finish on top of their various career ventures. 'I was a bit quiet,' she remembered. 'I never really had the drive to go any further. I danced until I was 18 or 19 but then I lost interest. I think dancing is a hard life but I loved it while I was doing it.'

Perhaps, some have speculated, the reason for her losing interest in dancing was that she had fallen in love, soon after the day she first met Ronald Charles Minogue, commonly known as Ron. He was a trainee accountant, and his roots were not a million miles away from Carol's, as his family hailed from Ireland. He married Carol when she was 20 and the happy couple moved to Melbourne so Ron could look for a new job to support the family they were planning to build. Ron had always been a laidback and serious man. He and Carol were a very happy couple as they entered married life. Music was a part of their household – they were fans of both the Rolling Stones and the Beatles – but they could not have been described as music fanatics.

Dannii was the couple's third and final child. Kylie arrived in 1968, followed by Brendan a year later. Then, two years later, on 20 October 1971, Carol once more gave birth, this time to another girl, Danielle Jane. Some of those who were to share the pop charts with Dannii were also born that year including future Take That singer and songwriting genius Gary Barlow, British easy-listening pop star Dido, American singers Missy Elliott and Fred Durst, rappers Tupac Shakur and Lisa Lopes, and Latino star Ricky Martin. Meanwhile, Rod Stewart was topping the British singles charts that day with his now-legendary song 'Maggie May' and the album charts with *Every Picture Tells a Story*.

Dannii is a Libran, and the characteristics associated with Librans by those who believe in astrology certainly ring true in Dannii's case. They include a love of the arts and a desire for popularity. Librans are also said to have a higher-than-usual interest in beauty and personal appearance, which again matches Dannii very well. And she not only believes in astrology but also studies it keenly, as she once outlined to an interviewer. 'I'm a Libra, but it's your rising sign that's your character and I'm Scorpio rising. Libra likes balance and harmony. I always strive for that. I like things to be nice. The Scorpio is very strong, very protective – very self-protective.'

Other famous Librans include actress and singer Julie Andrews, Beatle John Lennon and 'iron lady' politician Margaret Thatcher. Having been considered something of an 'iron lady' herself, Dannii is considered by some to have been cut from the same cloth as her fellow Libran Thatcher. As we shall see, Dannii is focused and ambitious but actually a very warm character.

The children spent part of their childhood in the Surrey Hills district of Melbourne. As with several streets in the quiet suburb, including Durham, Essex and Suffolk, the suburb itself is named after an English county. However, the family were often on the move and so the children got to know many different Melbourne suburbs during their upbringing. This mobility meant it was an extra challenge for them to make and maintain friendships. They spent a long time in the leafy, middle-class Canterbury suburb, where Ron had secured a job in the accountancy department of the local council. They had various pets including a goldfish, a terrapin (which was to eventually eat the goldfish – a memorably upsetting day for the children) and a big black dog called Bitsa. They also had a cat called Pussy, but Dannii was not a fan of it. 'Pussy was actually a family cat, but because Kylie was the eldest it was kind of her pet really. She was this huge, fat, stroppy, chocolate-coloured thing that lived to a ripe old age. She just used to sit there and look at you. I remember her sitting on top of the garage and planning attacks on the dog. She used to run in the mud, and then go, "Mmm, muddy feet," and just walk slowly across the car from front to back. She was a vile cat.'

Dannii quickly established herself as an outgoing and energetic member of the family. She was closest in age to her brother and this gave her a rather laddish outlook on life, which, as we shall see, continues to this day. Back then, she had something of the tomboy about her, and has a scar to prove it. 'I've got one on my leg from hurtling down a hill on a BMX bike, trying to go faster than my brother,' she said. 'The pedal came off, and I went to put my foot down but the wire thing the pedal was attached to cut right down my leg.' Even the photographs of her childhood attest to this aspect of Dannii's personality. 'In every baby picture, I'm carrying a frog, covered in mud, holding a truck in the other hand, with a BMX beside me, but I love being the baby,' she said. 'I'm a sucker for being cuddled and pampered.'

The Minogue family albums also betray a slightly harsh reality about Dannii's place in the family. As the youngest of three children, she was less of a novelty. 'I remember being slightly peeved when I looked through the baby photo albums,' she has admitted. 'It goes Kylie, five million; Brendan, five thousand; me, five. It really was the youngest-child thing, unfortunately.' The photographs that do exist build into an overall portrait of a lively girl. 'There are pictures of me on my BMX covered in mud, riding down a hill,' she said. 'Then, I think, at about the time I discovered Olivia Newton-

John, the girl thing kicked in. Kylie was always a girly girl. I'm tomboyish, she's princessy.'

She was a precocious kid, too, and the sense of perfection that she has become so known for was evident from an early age. 'I was a strange child – at my computer till 11.30pm making an essay perfect,' she said. 'My father used to drag me away. My brother and sister weren't academic at all. It would be blissful to not care, but I can't.'

A career-obsessed woman, Dannii has always been more than willing to put in the hours to make everything as perfect as it can be. She and Kylie would follow similar career paths and go on to become globally famous, both starring on television and in the pop charts. However, Dannii insists, they are less two peas in a pod, more chalk and cheese. 'We are complete opposites,' she once said of herself and Kylie. She later emphasised, 'Kylie and I are completely black and white, salt and pepper.' It is true in so many ways. One of the key ways in which Dannii differs from her sister is in her highly outspoken nature. 'She's said to me, "I wish I could say what I want to say." But she just clams up and can't speak at all if there's something she's passionate about. I'm the opposite. I've got myself into trouble a lot of times because I say what I think. I'm very open, very honest. It's important to me to be truthful, but I don't mean to hurt anyone. In fact, the only person I hurt is myself. I'm trying to curb what I say because I don't want to deal with hurting myself.'

That outspoken way was evident from early in Dannii's life and, as we shall repeatedly see, has not left her. Indeed, arguably, it has increased the more her fame has grown, and ultimately helped bring her to the attention of a man who is famed for his own very outspoken ways, bringing her increased fame and fortune as a result.

As a child, she shared a bedroom with Kylie, and even here their competitive natures showed. 'We put a sticky-tape line down the middle at one point,' said Dannii.

Dannii was also the more confident of the two sisters during their childhoods and sometimes her enthusiasm would be unfairly mistaken for arrogance. Back then, though, she was too busy having fun with her brother and more often her sister. Minogue duets have been only occasional events since the girls became famous, but they regularly happened when they were kids growing up. Dannii and her big sister performed together in the family home, singing songs by Swedish pop group ABBA and tunes from the hit musical *Grease* to their impressed parents and brother. Holding hairbrushes in their hands as pretend microphones, they were like so many children who dream of pop stardom. But Dannii and her big sister were already hinting that they had a special talent, and for them those commonplace childhood dreams would eventually come true, and in some style. Dannii was already daring to dream big. When she was seven years of age, she sat down to watch the famous musical *Grease* and it was to leave a huge and lasting impression on her. Two hours after she sat down, she got up again full of excitement and renewed fantasies. 'I loved the film,' she recalled. 'All of the singing and dancing. I was only seven but at that age you're so impressionable.'

Kylie too was beginning to focus her eyes on the prize. Both Dannii and her big sister started taking singing and dancing lessons. This was not as a result of any 'pushy parent' pressure in the family home. 'I was never very keen on them taking up dancing because I knew how hard it was,' said Carol of her two daughters. She was, though, supportive. 'But when they started I didn't try to stop them because I had to let them do what they felt was right. I wanted them to learn the piano because I think the piano is something that you have for life. As for singing, I can't sing a note. I couldn't even sing in church,' she admitted.

Dannii, though, was clear about her dream even down to the visuals of it, and said that it was one widely shared by her contemporaries. 'When I was growing up in Australia every little girl wanted to look like Olivia Newton-John, but now I'd hate to be blonde; it wouldn't feel like me,' she said. 'Having said that, I often go out in blonde wigs. I take after my dad in having dark-brown hair. Kylie takes after my mum.'

She also has other non-entertainment memories of her childhood, including happy trips to the beach with Brendan and Kylie to watch fairy penguins come ashore as the sun set at the end of the day. They and their parents would be almost the only people watching and these were magical times for the family as they encountered cute wonders of nature. Since then, that beach has become a crowded and popular tourist destination. Dannii feels this has spoiled its charm, which makes her childhood memories all the more precious and rare. Another early joy came in 1980, when the Minogue family travelled to Britain for a holiday. They visited relatives in Wales and also took a sightseeing trip around London, the city that Dannii would later make her home. As she looked round London, Dannii's eyes were wide open with awe.

Hers was a liberal, relaxed and progressive childhood. There was no element of religion forced on her and she credits this with her attitude to life. 'I don't know if it's because I was never brought up with religion in the house, but I don't have closeted ideas about what I was allowed, and not allowed, to do,' she said. 'Not to say that I'm a wild girl, but I do get confused about being able to go to an art gallery and admire a nude, but, if you take a photo of a nude body, which is the modern equivalent of an oil painting, it's offensive. My parents let me make up my own mind about things. They'd say, "That's your opinion, and not everybody is going to feel the same way." But they knew how important it was for me to think for myself.'

The first music she heard was on records. 'The first records I heard were my parents' ones that I played, which were, like, Stevie Wonder, Boz Scaggs,' she said. 'By the time I was into buying my own records, I was buying Olivia Newton-John, *Grease* soundtrack, and all that kind of stuff. I'd be listening to it, thinking, Wow, isn't that fantastic. I have to make a record!'

She had the performance bug in her and so there was going to be no holding her back. From the start, Dannii was hardworking and willing to sweat to get where she wanted to be. She affects a humble stance when discussing her abilities back then. 'As much as people think I'm pushy, I fell into it,' she said. 'I've seen footage of Christina Aguilera when she was about seven years old and she was singing like she does now. I wasn't like that.'

At the tender age of seven, she would perform to a national television audience when she landed a small role on an Australian television series after a family friend who worked at the Crawford Productions company suggested Dannii and Kylie come in for a screen test. They had a family connection with the company in the shape of their Auntie Suzette, who worked there. Both girls landed small parts on a show called *The Sullivans*. The programme was set during the Second World War and focused on the Sullivan family, who lived in Camberwell, Victoria. The 30-minute episodes were broadcast on the Nine Network from 1976. The final episode was broadcast in 1983, but by then the programme had an international following. The ITV network had bought it for a mid-afternoon slot at the turn of the decade, before it moved to a midday airing. Even without Dannii's involvement in the programme, the significance of *The Sullivans* to the future career of herself and Kylie is important. The popularity of *The Sullivans* among UK viewers paved the way for the subsequent wave of Australian dramas to be shown here, including *Sons and Daughters* and *The Young Doctors*. In turn, the popularity of those daytime programmes led to *Neighbours* and *Home and Away* – the shows that made Dannii and her sister so famous – being broadcast in the UK.

Dannii played a character called Carla in a scene portraying a soldier's dream. Carla – a Dutch orphan – had previously been played by Kylie but Dannii got the nod when the part had to be reprised after Kylie left the show. This was something of a belated triumph for Dannii, who had been initially earmarked to audition for the part. Kylie had gone along to the audition with Dannii and Carol only at the last moment, and, although Dannii auditioned well for the role, she was a little too young to play Carla, and Kylie nipped in to land the role. So it was with glee that Dannii eventually got to play Carla, albeit only in a brief dream.

But both sisters would soon also appear in another Crawford show. *Skyways* was set in a busy international airport, called the Pacific International Airport, and followed the lives of those who worked there. It included some controversial storylines, particularly for the era in which it was made, including lesbian characters and gritty murder plots. *Skyways* was strong on cliffhangers, with the theme for each episode briefly set up at the end of the previous instalment. It was first broadcast on 9 July 1979, and had a regular slot of 9.30pm, reflecting its sometimes adult themes (although, during subsequent reruns on Australian and British television, it was broadcast in afternoon slots, gritty scenes and all.)

It was a cheap and cheerful affair. Kylie remembered, 'We have a plane crash. You can see the tissue paper on the model plane as they're rocking it. In one scene another character asks me something and you can see that I have absolutely no idea what I'm supposed to do.'

A significant event did occur for her, though, when one day she noticed a boy who was 'really chubby with a bowl haircut'. His name? Jason Donovan.

Dannii again followed Kylie, when she also won a brief part in this low-budget drama. But then the tables would turn, and it would be Kylie who would trail in her wake for a while, as Dannii was soon to become one of the most famous children in Australia. Between the ages of 10 and 17, Dannii was television royalty in Australia.

Dannii began singing and acting lessons at the Johnny Young Talent School. She worked hard and was soon picked out of the pack to appear on *Young Talent Time*. She was by no means an obvious choice, as the dance teachers had told her. 'I knew I was bad,' Minogue says, 'but I loved it so much and I hung on every moment, every word the teacher was saying. But they chose me and they told me afterwards, "You were absolutely the worst, but we loved your enthusiasm and knew we could harness that and train you." From that I came to learn every moment is precious and fun.' Indeed, this is a self-realisation that Dannii has kept in mind to this day. 'I know there are more talented performers than me. I know that for sure,' Minogue admits. 'So I'm a very lucky woman on a winning streak, and I'll do the best I can. If my best isn't good enough, then I've still had an amazing shot at it. Every day, and I say this at the risk of sounding blunt, I can't believe they're still letting me do this.'

She quickly became a darling of the Australian public, described as 'one of the biggest household names in Australia'. One Aussie journalist described her image on the show: 'treacle-sweet personality, a soft, calm voice and gentle manner she simply oozes "niceness".'

Those who make the assumption that Dannii has coat-tailed on Kylie's success do so in blissful ignorance of just how massive this show was in Australia and just how central to its success Dannii was. Kylie would land a guest slot on it one day but she mostly could only watch from the sidelines as Dannii became the first truly famous Minogue sister. And Kylie quickly became used to – as she had to – being known as Dannii Minogue's sister. She was routinely introduced to people this way and ultimately took to introducing herself as such. Dannii remembered, 'Kylie wasn't famous at that stage, and she was always called "Dannii's sister". She hated that, because she was the oldest child and it was at a time in her life when she was developing her own personality. She didn't want to be defined by me.'

But, according to those who knew her then, it was a normal sister relationship and there was no real resentment. 'There was no hint of jealousy,' said one of Kylie's first boyfriends. 'The impression I got was that they were great mates and that she was quite enthused about it.'

She was even more enthused when she was given a guest slot on the show. She joined her famous sister on the stage and together they sang – perhaps inevitably – the Eurythmics/Aretha Franklin song 'Sisters Are Doing it for Themselves'. It was a lively and eye-catching performance. For Kylie it was the only time she appeared on the show, but for Dannii it was business as usual the following week. She was a key part of the show and was absolutely loved by both the crew and the viewers. As her friend Sam Buckley recalled, 'All the boys fancied her, all the girls aspired to look like her – she was the one.'

'Dannii was *so* popular,' recalled one of the dancers who appeared on the show. 'I can't believe Dannii has not made it as big as Kylie. She was always the favourite on *YTT*.'

The cast of the programme would sometimes 'go on tour' and Carol would be at Dannii's side on these jaunts. She could be seen at every performance, proudly watching from the audience. She encouraged Dannii but was careful to never put pressure on her or Kylie. She wanted them to chase their dreams and was happy when they found success. But she wanted them to know that they were loved and could be happy whether they made it or not.

Notwithstanding this, Dannii was absolutely determined to make it and was working very hard to ensure she did just that. She was simultaneously making sure her academic efforts were also strenuous. 'Every night after school I would go to work at the television studio,' she said. 'Every Saturday I would dance for 12 hours. But at the same time I refused to give up at school. I wasn't prepared to let my schoolwork suffer. Every lunchtime I would sit with the nerds in the library and do my homework. I was very studious. A straight-As student ... Sometimes I got A-pluses.

'I think our parents helped us to prepare for this sort of life because from a very early stage they have let us make our own decisions and bear the responsibility for them.'

Again, there is clearly a sense that her family gave her a very positive grounding to pursue the ambitions she wanted. Hers was a supportive home but in no sense a pushy one. She was encouraged in an appropriate way. They also kept an eye on her finances – not that she had much time to squander her earnings. 'Most of the years I was earning I had nothing to spend money on,' she explained. 'I worked six days a week and, on Sundays, I did my homework ... Mum and Dad would have let me blow it at the games parlour if I wanted to ... But, however weird and out there I might seem, in how I look and what I do I'm pretty conservative.'

It was at this stage that she began considering her image keenly. Although she has long been advised by some fine minds, Dannii is also fortunate to have an almost instinctual grasp of how to build an image. Accordingly, she was about to make a major alteration to her image. She was still known as Danielle at this time, but not for much longer. She soon changed it to Dannii. 'I changed it because everyone was pronouncing it incorrectly,' she said. 'Lots of people called me Dannell instead of Danielle. Dannii is shorter and easier to say.'

However, this change brought some new complications, as it was routinely misspelled as Dani, Danii and Dannie. Furthermore, she was much later to become embroiled in a controversy surrounding an *X Factor* contestant who suffered himself from a similar issue of varying pronunciations of his name.

Her passage to *Young Talent Time* had been a no-brainer for Dannii, but her mother and father were not immediately convinced by the move. 'When they asked me to go on, my parents were very worried, because, once you're in, you're in,' she said. 'Like the contestants on *X Factor*, it changes your life for ever. But it wasn't a question for me. I definitely wanted to do it.' But Dannii was also aware of the knock-on effect that her new commitment would have on those closest to her. 'It was also tough on the rest of the family because I had rehearsals five days a week after school and worked 12 hours a day on a Saturday for six years. I needed my parents to take me there and it was a large commitment for them. The hardest aspect for them was to get me to all those things and still have enough time for the other children in the family.' When she got there she was amused by much of what she found. She remembers, 'There were all these other kids in full show-time makeup and hideous outfits with sequins, all desperately wanting to be chosen. I really didn't care that much about it. I just went along because I enjoyed it, but I knew I couldn't sing or dance so I didn't think I'd ever have a chance.'

Away from all this entertainment-world ambition, Dannii was going through the changes that any girl does in her teenage years. These included an increasing tendency to notice the opposite sex – this comes with its charms but also its challenges. One day she had a very embarrassing moment on a beach while trying to put a vain man in his place. 'I was with a group of girlfriends walking along an Australian mall in our bathers; we'd just come off the beach,' she recalled with a wince. 'This guy was standing posing, thinking he was the greatest. I yelled to my friends, "Oh, God, what a poser," and walked straight into a pole.'

But there were more successful experiences for the teenage Dannii. She was a famous, talented and successful girl and as such had no shortage of admirers, even if some of them were too shy to approach her. Her first boyfriend is somebody she remembers to this day. 'He was called Gary and he lived in Sydney while I lived in Melbourne, which wasn't exactly handy. I was about 14 and met him through a friend. I often used to fly to Sydney to see him because at that time I was working in a TV show called *Young Talent Time*, which meant travelling all around Australia. I've been working in show business since I was ten, so I grew up fast.' She continued with her schooling, too. 'My best subjects were computers, maths and science,' she said. Dannii was also learning things at home, her parents teaching her and her two siblings many lessons for life. 'My parents taught us to be very independent, to make our own choices and to be careful about who we work with. They taught me to listen to other people's advice, then listen to yourself and go with your own instinct. My father's an accountant and he's taught me to handle my own finances.'

Kylie was still very much in Dannii's shadow at this stage. Not only was she routinely referred to as 'Dannii's sister', but she also would often be asked to help Dannii out with answering fan mail, often having to deal with hundreds of requests each week.

Meanwhile, Dannii was living the dream on *Young Talent Time*. She loved working there, even when handed some rather hair-raising tasks to perform on air. 'They had these segments where they'd bring on animals and ask who wanted to hold them,' she recalled. 'When it was a snake, I'd always be like, "Me, me." From the moment I picked one up, I loved them. I like dangerous animals.'

Soon, though, it was time for Dannii to fly the *YTT* nest. That was an emotional day not just for her and the crew of the show but also for television viewers across Australia. She had come close to being a national institution over the past six years and there were tears on set as her reign came to an end. 'Good night, Australia,' she said, choking back the tears.

The next stage of Dannii's incredible career was an acting part. At 16, she landed a part in Channel Nine's latest period drama *All the Way*. This was to be Dannii's most substantial drama part to date and therefore an exciting but somewhat nerve-racking challenge for her. She had attended the audition only for the experience of the auditioning process, rather than with any special hope of landing the part. However, that is exactly what she did.

Her character was called Penelope Seymour, who was an embittered and sexually experienced teenager, the daughter of unaffectionate parents, one of whom was a politician. One critic described her character as 'snakey', another called Penny ' a scheming brat', but Dannii was even more direct in her assessment. 'She is a real bitch,' she said. A pilot miniseries of *All the Way* had gone out first and received largely negative reviews. Dannii started filming for the series proper in April 1988. 'It's great fun,' she giggled at the time. But soon, she complained, she was being asked to take part in 'some really awful scenes'. She was finding it hard to truly relate to her character, although she could sympathise with some aspects of her. 'I know someone who has similar characteristics, but I've taken bits and pieces from different people I know,' she said. 'She does have some close friends but she mainly has them to use. In a way I am like her in that when I believe in something strongly no one will get in my way. But neither to the extent she does nor for the same reasons.'

One of her co-stars was only too happy to offer her assistance and input. 'Rowena Wallace has given me some help,' Dannii said of the actress who played her onscreen mother. 'She's made some suggestions on how Penny would react to something.'

But, for her first major acting part, she was having to learn the hard way that there were few shortcuts when it came to performing this way. 'There's no easy way out,' she said. 'There is so much involved, so much to learn.'

In the first few months of the run of *All the Way*, Dannii learned the harsh ways of viewing figures as the show performed badly in the ratings. It was then moved to a weekly slot. Dannii was in no mood to give up and continued trying her utmost at the craft. 'This is my debut, I want to show I can act,' she said. The Australian newspaper the *Herald* was not convinced she could. 'Unfortunately, Minogue (playing wayward teenager Penelope Seymour) cannot act at all and, at 16, looks like Joan Collins' little sister,' wrote its television critic Gay Alcorn. 'She plays the sexy boyfriend-stealer, fluttering her eyelids, pouting and seducing her teacher. The Human Rights and Equal Opportunity Commission should be called in for sexism verging on the criminal.' She could perhaps have drawn some comfort from the fact that the review was equally damning about almost every aspect of the show. '*All the Way* does not have a clue what it's supposed to be doing. It mixes standard teenage love stories, with their presumed titillation value, with quite serious social issues.' Alcorn concluded with a thundering: '*All the Way* insults everybody.' But, other than that, you liked it – right?

Again, though, she was in the ascendancy. From her small roles in *The Sullivans* and *Skyways*, she was now taking a larger acting part on the small screen, which was a positive step up. She also appeared, in July 1988, in the television variety show *New Generation*. However, by this time, Kylie had become a hugely famous figure, thanks to her part in *Neighbours*. Having followed in Kylie's footsteps in *The Sullivans* and *Skyways*, Dannii had left her sister trailing in her wake in the fame stakes with her *Young Talent Time* profile. But Kylie had now risen higher than either sister had before. The Minogue name was already famous in Australia thanks to Dannii, but now Kylie had made it a familiar name in other countries around the world as well. Dannii, already a canny operator, was more than adequately equipped to propel herself to new heights herself.

CHAPTER TWO

closer each day

During the middle of the 1980s, a new television show was to arrive in England that would make our viewing nation all the more enamoured of Australia and its people. On 18 March 1985, a new drama programme was broadcast on Australia's Seven Network. It had an inauspicious start and struggled along with poor ratings for four months before it was cancelled. Nobody would have predicted at that point that the show would be resurrected, become an enormous success and be the launch pad for Kylie to become globally famous and – ultimately – Dannii to become the same. To tell the story of how *Neighbours* became such a hit, we must return briefly to 1980 when two programmes were aired that provided a spark of inspiration. The Australian television network Seven commissioned two drama pilots. One was called *A*

Special Place and dealt with an elderly woman's relationship with some homeless children. Then came a show called *People Like Us*, which followed the fortunes of five families living on one street. Neither show was commissioned for a series but both concepts, particularly the second one, remained of interest in Australian television circles and eventually prompted the creation of *Neighbours*.

It was a man called Reg Watson who came up with the idea for *Neighbours* (originally titled *One Way Street*), a daily soap set in a fictional suburb called Erinsborough on a cul-de-sac named Ramsay Street. Watson had form, having also launched such shows as *Prisoner: Cell Block H* and *The Young Doctors* in Australia and *Crossroads* in Britain. Grundy Television was the production company and, although its cancellation after just four months on air was a blow, they kept the faith and began negotiations with other networks, including Ten. That network took it and production moved to Nunawading. The essential format remained the same with the new network but a few improvements were made ahead of its relaunch in January 1986. Chief among these were that more airtime should be devoted to the younger characters. Four months into its new life, *Neighbours* introduced a new character called Charlene. During an early scene in her incumbency, she punched another character called Scott in the face after wrongly assuming he was a burglar. It was an unlikely start for a romance that would grip viewers across the world, for Scott was played by Jason Donovan and Charlene was played by Kylie Minogue. Their romance would be the key factor in the success that *Neighbours* was to enjoy.

Jan Russ was the casting director who hired Kylie, who had already appeared in a television miniseries called *The Henderson Kids* and another in a children's television programme called *The Zoo Family*. She had watched her appear in *The Zoo Family* and, noting her 'extra charisma', thought she would be perfect to play the part of Charlene. There was plenty of competition for the part, with more than 40 other actresses vying for the role. But Russ was insistent that it had to go to Kylie because, she said, 'the camera loved her'. Originally, the character was going to appear for only 13 weeks in the show but, once Kylie and Donovan had built up their on-camera chemistry, the programme makers were never going to let her slip out of their grasp. Donovan described the rapport he built up with Kylie as a once-in-a-million occurrence. The programme was becoming a hit, thanks in part also to the clever marketing strategy of taking the cast around shopping centres across the country to help whip up extra excitement. Soon the fans were flocking to filming locations, with the frenzy they created being compared to Beatlemania. 'We were trying to get work done with all these screaming kids,' recalled a crew member. The fanbase was fierce and loyal – and was about to become international. The excitement in Australia was to be reflected in Britain, too.

In October 1986, *Neighbours* first hit the airwaves in Britain. It had a lunchtime slot on BBC1 but became so popular among schoolchildren that a repeat was demanded and duly scheduled in the early-evening slot. The sunshine of Australia was proving popular in contrast to the more dull domestic shows such as *Coronation Street* and *Emmerdale*. 'They are quite dour, heavy and suppressed shows, whereas *Neighbours* was more uplifting,' said *Neighbours* actor Stefan Dennis, who played Scott's brother Paul.

The storyline between Charlene and Scott continued to enrapture the viewing public and, when the couple married in Episode 523 (broadcast in July 1987), the excitement was enormous. More than 4,000 fans turned up to try to watch the scenes being shot in Australia.

But, much as Kylie was enjoying the newfound fame *Neighbours* offered her, she quickly outgrew the show with its tacky plots and lack of authenticity. Within 18 months of her first appearance, she was shooting her final scene. Her character was last seen driving away to Queensland, where a new life awaited her. Kylie was given a framed montage of magazine cover shoots she had done as a leaving present. There had been plenty of such covers, as *Neighbours* had made her internationally famous and launched her music career. The world was taking notice of her, and one person who was taking notice of Kylie's fame was her sister Dannii.

Home and Away was first aired on the Seven Network in January 1988, as Kylie was already preparing to leave

Neighbours. Having let *Neighbours* slip through its fingers to Ten, Seven was keen to make *Home and Away* a hit. Head of drama Alan Bateman created a winning pilot and the show was commissioned to rival *Neighbours*. Bateman had come up with the concept for *Home and Away* during a visit to a small country town. He noticed a new building being constructed and discovered it was to be a foster home for children. Further investigation revealed to him that some local residents were bitterly opposed to such an institution being built in their neighbourhood. Here, he felt, was potential for some television magic. 'There was a great deal of conflict in the town over it. It had all the elements of a fine drama,' he said.

Toughened, streetwise children would grapple with a new life in a peaceful, family area. He had in mind a more gritty affair than *Neighbours*. While *Home and Away* was never to be the edgiest of dramas, it did have attention-grabbing storylines. Launched on 17 January 1988, in its first 13 years on air alone it showed 10 weddings, 12 pregnancies, 2 miscarriages and 11 deaths. The success of the show can be shown in another statistic from the same timeframe: it won eight Logie Awards, with four consecutive wins for Most Popular Series from 1993 to 1996. By 2001, it was being televised in around 50 countries, including New Zealand, Canada, Ireland, Norway, Israel, Dubai, Botswana, South Africa and Zimbabwe.

Dannii had been a key factor in this success, though

she joined the show relatively deep into its history. She first appeared in Episode 400. Her part was as Emma Jackson, the niece of popular and longstanding leading character Ailsa Roberts. Emma was a rebellious, punky tomboy teenager. It is fair to say that, in every way, Dannii's *Home and Away* experience was to be something of a pale shadow of the success Kylie enjoyed both on and as a result of *Neighbours*. Whereas Kylie's Charlene character became almost instantly and massively popular, Dannii's Emma was never warmed to in the same way and never achieved anything approaching the iconic status of Charlene. Kylie was on fire at this point, winning four awards at the prestigious Logie Awards in April 1988, including becoming the youngest ever person to win the gold. Moreover, *Home and Away* was always somewhat in the shadow of *Neighbours*. But Dannii was to spend one year on the Summer Bay soap, and become a familiar face in the UK as a result.

Ahead of her first appearance as Emma, whom we first see on the show wearing a leather jacket and torn jeans, she said she was 'absolutely thrilled' to land the part. 'She's had a rough life being mistreated by her father and so gets herself into a lot of trouble,' Dannii says. 'She ends up in a remand centre and, because she can't go back home, the only relative she can find is Ailsa, her aunt, so she goes to live with her. Emma is a real rebel so she'll be a great character to play. This is only the second real acting job I've done, so I think it will be a good series to get into, particularly because it's going so well in the UK, too.'

It was indeed going well: 11.5 million Brits tuned in every day and Dannii was of particular interest in Blighty because Kylie was already a popular figure here. When *Home and Away* got beefy *Neighbours* star Craig McLachlan, it was another boost.

On her opening day of filming it became clear to Dannii what a tight budget some aspects of the production were on. It was filmed in Sydney's Channel Seven studios and at Palm Beach, and it was not without its bloopers. 'The funniest thing happened in one of my first scenes,' Dannii revealed. 'In the beginning, Emma was really arrogant and punk and in every scene she would slam the door when she walked in or out. So I walked in and I slammed the door and everything fell off the wall on the set. I was so embarrassed and scared and so nervous about what everyone would say, but everyone just packed up laughing.'

She was laughing too as her fame soared. Just as *Home and Away* was the – slightly – edgier cousin of *Neighbours*, so too was Dannii seen as the slightly more out-there Minogue sister due to the character she played and her slightly less girl-next-door look. She had to back-comb her hair to get into character and soon complained that this, together with the regular dyeing, was ruining her hair. Although she was not warmed to in the same way as Kylie and her Charlene character had been, female viewers had noticed this spunky, sassy girl and male viewers were admiring her for their own reasons.

The media were interested too. Famous siblings have always found that their individual profile is considerably boosted as a result of their relative. So at this time Dannii came under increased press attention, something she had dealt with herself during her *Young Talent Time* days and something she had also watched her sister deal with fairly well. 'I guess I have learned a few things from what Kylie has been through,' Dannii told a reporter at the time. 'It does change your life. If you are in magazines every week it changes your life – everyone knows who you are.'

As with her *All the Way* character, she felt she was essentially different from the part she played. Again, though, she could relate to the character. 'I'm a placid person,' Dannii said. 'But I know a few people a bit like Emma. And as an actress you learn to pick up people's movements and reactions.' She was becoming a bit tired of the inevitable comparisons that were made between her and her sister. 'We're different people,' she replied when a press reporter raised the issue with her. '*Home and Away* is a different programme, on a different network with different characters,' she added pointedly.

Her character softened up as the run went on. She had plenty of love interests, including with Grant Mitchell, the character played by ex-*Neighbours* pin-up Craig McLachlan. His presence was helping the show's popularity, as was that of the high-cheekboned hunk that is Guy Pearce, who has since gone on to have a successful career in big movies. She said the cast were unaware as they filmed the show how huge it had become in Britain. 'We had no concept,' she said. 'We had no idea how … people cut school to run home and watch it. I just thought it was a bit weird and wacky how you were so into this show. For us, in Australia, it was popular but it was one of many shows.'

After a year, she was ready to leave the show. She had grown up during her time on *Home and Away* and it was inevitable that there would be a parting of the way in time. By the time she left, *Home and Away* was well on its way to knocking *Neighbours* off its perch. When it reached its 1,000th episode in 1992, it was getting more viewers than its old rival. Not that all were so impressed. The London *Evening Standard*'s acerbic television critic, Victor Lewis-Smith, wrote a storming condemnation of it. 'The folk who live in Summer Bay are cardboard cut-outs, leading one-dimensional lives in a place so pedestrian it makes Clacton look like Las Vegas,' he wrote. 'Even the title lacks imagination: *Home and Away*, a meaningless pairing of opposites – it might just as well be called *Left and Right* or *Yes and No* – embracing everything but defining nothing.'

Perhaps Dannii was getting out at the right time. In her final episode, Emma Jackson was as tetchy as ever. Her foster father Alf was angry with her for slinking off to the city for a job interview without telling him and his wife Ailsa first. He ticks her off but Emma is in no mood to accept the punishment. She resents being treated like a naughty child and storms off, never to be seen again. But, of course, thanks to the fame she acquired on *Home and Away*, Dannii herself was to be seen much more widely in future.

Looking back on the show, she was generally proud and happy with her time in Summer Bay. She was honest too. When asked in 2001 what the biggest fashion *faux pas* of her life to date had been, she replied, 'Probably the school uniform in *Home and Away*.'

She had grown up while on the show and soon became wary of the price that was paid by the relentless pace inherent in making such a regular soap. 'You can't stay in that for ever – come on,' she said after leaving. 'I mean half the scripts didn't even make sense. I'd go into work and say, "That's completely different from what my character was saying last week." And they'd say, "Just get your bikini on, get on the beach, say the lines and no one will worry about it." '

It's true that the plots were frequently incredible, but for many of the soap's keenest fans that was often part of its appeal. 'The thing I like about *Home and Away* is how ridiculous and outlandish it is,' said an Irish fan-club member. 'The characters are living in a parallel universe – you can be hit by lightning nine times and no one will bat an eyelid. And there are so many mineshafts falling in and floods hitting the town.'

For Dannii, though, it was definitely time to move on. In fact, she was shocked that some people – such as the actors who played her onscreen parents – had stayed for so long in Summer Bay. 'There were people who had been on *Home and Away* for eight years and I just couldn't understand it,' she said. 'Whatever I'm doing I want to feel I'm learning something new.'

And for Dannii something new meant launching her own fashion label. 'I started off just designing costumes for myself,' she said. 'I got amazing feedback. I've always liked designing, but never had any formal training. I like to learn about new things. Terry, my manager, was able to set it up so I thought, Why not? Let's do it. I just find things I like, and I've been lucky enough to be able to utilise them and get the opportunity to do it. I mean, if I was just Dannii that no one had ever heard of before, there'd be no way I could ever have my own fashion label.'

She was on a roll and people were starting to sit up and take notice of the younger Minogue girl again. 'Just look at Dannii now' was the headline of an admiring article in the *Sunday Mail*. Just look at Dannii indeed. When her first fashion range was launched in K-Mart stores throughout Australia in September 1988, it had sold out in under two weeks.

The summer range was followed by the 'high summer' range, which was admired by the *Sunday Tasmanian*. Louise Bower positively purred over the garments that made up the second Dannii range. '[There are] large oversized tops, T-shirts with turtle necks, keyhole-back tie tops, crop tops with the Danielle Minogue signature, plus many more styles. The bottoms to mix-or-match are equally variable – drawstring waist shorts, long-leg shorts with cuffs, bicycle shorts, and a little cotton mini. The entire collection is made in Australia and there is nothing in the range costing more than $17.98. The colours are Dannii's favourites ... amber, lime, hot pink, and of course plenty of black-and-white. All styles come in sizes to fit girls from seven to 16 years.'

Kylie had by this point become a pop sensation. Having sung at events such as charity benefits – on one occasion alongside Dannii at an anti-drugs gig, where they sang 'Sisters are Doing it for Themselves' – she had entered the pop industry proper by releasing her first single. And the real surge was about to come. In July 1987, Dannii's big sister released her cover of 'The Locomotion'. It reached number one, spent seven weeks there and became the bestselling single of the 1980s in Australia. Then, she flew to London and signed up with the formidable songwriting team that was Stock Aitken Waterman. Her first single with the team was 'I Should Be So Lucky'. She was indeed striking lucky, the single reached number one in numerous countries including Britain, Australia, Germany, Finland, Hong Kong and Israel. She was quickly becoming pop royalty – and meeting real royalty. At Sydney's bicentennial celebrations she met the Prince and Princess of Wales. It was an exciting moment for her and she became tongue-tied with nerves. She was quickly breaking chart records. Her single 'Got To Be Certain' was the first single to go straight to number one in Australia and then her eponymous debut album made her the youngest ever female to hit the top of the UK album charts.

'The Locomotion' subsequently became a hit in Australia, where she became known as 'The Locomotion Girl'. On and on went Kylie's success, all of her first seven singles reached either number one or number two in the UK charts.

In 1989, Dannii was as proud and happy as any guest as Kylie celebrated her 21st birthday. There were 150 guests at the champagne bash at the Red Eagle Hotel in Sydney. The only slight shadow over the proceedings came when a bouncer overstepped the mark security-wise and shut out Jason Donovan.

Dannii, previously the more famous Minogue during her *Young Talent Time* days, had watched all this success with a mixture of pride and ambition. She liked what she saw and wanted a taste of it herself. By the time Kylie's seventh single, 'Wouldn't Change a Thing', was released, Dannii was already well on the way to launching her own pop career.

CHAPTER THREE

dannii

Although she was keen to emulate her sister's success in the music industry, Dannii was under absolutely no illusions that it was a tough business. Ever the straight-talking realist, she had already developed a strikingly jaded view of it simply by watching the experiences of Kylie. 'Everyone knows the music industry is drug-related – and you understand why when you see what happens to bands that come off the streets,' said Dannii once. 'It eats you up and spits you out. It's a business and people are out there to get what they can from you. If you end up in a psychiatric ward or a drug rehabilitation centre, they don't give a shit.'

These were cynical words from her about the industry she has had contrasting fortunes from, and it's little wonder, for she had watched as her sister was built up and then knocked down. Australia is a country not short on envy and its people are quick to hack away at anyone they believe has become a 'tall poppy'. While Kylie succeeded in the UK, Dannii was back home in Australia watching the tide turn against her sister in some quarters. 'After Kylie's experience, I get worried,' she said. 'I don't want to become really hard-nosed. People were wearing "I hate Kylie" T-shirts. I don't know what feelings she went through because we were three years apart and there's not much you can say on an overseas phone call. But I know she got really tough. She had to develop a hard face. And she was depressed for a really long time. But that was the extent of it. She's worked through that now. To me it was a jigsaw that didn't fit. People overseas were kissing her feet and loved her. And people in her own country hated her. When there are all those f***ed-up artists singing "Kill, Kill, Kill", how can you hate someone who sings pop music?'

She was also growing ever more cynical about the ways of the press photographers. 'If they behaved like humans, you wouldn't mind,' she said. 'But you try having your photograph taken when you get off the 23-hour flight from Melbourne – and then reading next day you looked really "daggy". They're a pack of dogs.' Given that a photograph of the Minogue sisters together represented such a lucrative target for such snappers, the two tended to travel separately whenever possible. 'It really annoys us to think a photographer might get £20,000 extra just for a picture of us together,' she said. 'We treat it like a joke, but it's not.'

Poor Dannii, a kind sister, she was sometimes moved to tears when considering the perception of her sister among the more envious sections of the Australian population. 'Kylie was probably the most successful to come out of Australia,' said Dannii, 'and Australians didn't know what to do. But look what she's done for this country. It's so sad the way she's been attacked, so disgusting. I don't see why. I've cried about it many times.'

She was keen to dispel at this point that her music career was not a new affair that she was embarking on off the back of her Summer Bay stardom. Quite the contrary, she insisted: it was actually a natural continuation of what was her obvious career path. It was the soap part that was the deviation, rather than vice versa, she insisted. 'Soaps don't launch you [in music],' she said firmly. 'It might look that way [to a lot of kids] at the moment. But I had six years of training at *YTT* [*Young Talent Time*]. Singing was my career but I was sitting around doing nothing after *YTT* and I got offered the show, and being hyperactive, I thought, Go for it. Obviously talent is involved but it's a lot of hard work. You need to know about the business. There's no books on it. You need a great agent or manager to get the parts. And you need the will and desire to do it.'

And, if anyone had the will and the desire to do it, it was Dannii. In January 1989, Dannii signed a contract with Mushroom Records. Within months she was busy recording what would become her debut album proper, and she reflected on the *Young Talent Time* albums she had previously worked on. 'Yeah, I did two *YTT* records, I think,' she said. 'They were done really quickly – like, just putting down a song somebody else had already done before. But that's not nearly as exciting as doing something completely new.'

It was indeed two *YTT* records she had worked on and her mildly dismissive description of them is actually fair enough. In 1985, she had recorded the well-known Madonna hit 'Material Girl' and it was released on the *YTT* album *Now and Then*. Two years later another *YTT* album was released called *Phenomenon*. This time it included two songs performed by Dannii. The first was the Europe rock track 'The Final Countdown' and the second was 'Let's Go' by the Cars. But these were her introduction to the process of recording serious music. She learned things about recording studios and honed her voice, which meant she was ahead of the game when it came to her more serious musical efforts later in life. All the same, recording solo music proper was to be a whole new ball game.

Dannii was so excited that, having signed up and confirmed the basic team for her album, she could hardly wait to get going. In the summer of 1989, she flew to Manhattan to start recording the material. As she did so, Dannii was in reflective mood about her life and that vital part of it – her career. Indeed, it became increasingly difficult to distinguish her career and life, such was her focus on the former. She said that her increasing public profile had led to her developing a thicker skin, a tendency she had observed at close quarters. 'You do get tougher,' she said. 'I saw it happen to Kylie. It's just one of those careers that you can never leave at work and so it becomes your whole life. I think our parents helped us to prepare for this sort of life because from a very early stage they have let us make our own decisions and bear the responsibility for them.'

This talk of her career becoming her whole life hinted yet again at a steely focus on the part of Dannii. As she was making the album, she gave an interview to a newspaper that once more laid demonstrated her fierce ambition. 'It's my ambition,' she said firmly of her dream to become a globally successful pop artist. 'It's what I want. I'm going to work hard to try to get it.'

Her plan sounded simple on paper: she wished to make an album of black American funk music that would become a hit first in Australia and she would then attempt to break into America. Along the way, she hoped, she could crack Europe and maybe Asia, too. It was a lofty ambition to hold but one she was confidently convinced she could and would pull off. 'America is a very difficult market to crack, whatever sort of music you're doing,' she said during an interview in a Manhattan hotel. 'But I'm in it now. I've started, and I will see it through.' Her steely determination was evident again when she explained how she had to persevere with her plan to record specifically a funk album in the face of a doubting record company. 'At the time, they thought I was crazy ... they said no one listens to that kind of music,' she explained. 'Because there was no chart evidence to show that the music was popular, I just asked them to trust me. Then, not long after I started recording, funk acts like Paula Abdul started getting into the top five charts in Australia.'

So these were fortuitous times for Dannii as her hunch about the music market received a degree of vindication. They were eye-opening times too, as she recorded with Alvin Moody and Vinnie Bell, two celebrated funk producers who were from New York's feared Bronx district. They had worked with Neneh Cherry, who was a major hit in the 1980s with catchy songs such as 'Buffalo Stance'. Each day, she would be driven to Moody's Bronx home for recording sessions and here her quest for authenticity was to be tested. First, she had to find someone willing to drive her there. As she quickly discovered, many taxi drivers would not even take her to the Bronx. Some drivers told her that, even though they had worked in New York for years, they had never visited that area out of fear of running into trouble in the tough streets. Once she did manage to get a lift there, she had an eye-opening experience, as she later recalled. 'We were driving up there and went through Harlem and all these guys were looking at me in the car,' she said. 'There were no white people around. I felt really strange, the odd person out. They made me feel different just by the way they were looking at me.'

For her, though, these eye-opening experiences were more than worth it to get the sound she wanted and to be guaranteed a degree of that all-too-valuable commodity: creative independence. There had been no keener student of Kylie's musical career than her sister. Dannii admired Kylie for what she had achieved but was also mindful of taking her own path, a path informed by the negatives Kylie had experienced along her own route. During an interview with the *Sun Herald*, Dannii said, 'There were lessons there. I find producers who listen to what I say. Kylie had years of recording with Stock, Aitken.' And, despite her unnerving experience of the Bronx, as long as she was being listened to by her studio colleagues Dannii was more than happy.

She had chosen to record in New York for one main reason, she explained. 'That's where we found the best producers for me,' she said. 'It worked out really well because I was able to get away from Australia and listen to the new sounds coming through in New York, which is more ahead than we are in that [funk-based music] field.' Of her two producers she said, 'I'm the first white artist they've worked with. They've previously worked with Neneh Cherry, Orange "Juice" Jones, Blue Magic and heaps more. We looked all around the world for producers for the music that I wanted to do. We didn't go to Stock, Aitken and Waterman because that's not anywhere near the style that we [Dannii and her manager] wanted to do.'

Dannii was keen to be involved in the writing as well

as recording and she co-wrote one track, 'Party Jam', with producers Alvin Moody and Vinnie Bell. 'I'd never written any lyrics before and desperately wanted to,' she said. 'I sat down and thought, OK, I'm gonna write, and then I got a mental block and thought, Oh, I can't think of anything to write, and so I fell asleep and woke up with all these lyrics in my head and I thought, What will I do?, so I wrote them down and took them in the next day.' However, she found the process of actually handing them over to the producers an excruciating experience to say the least. 'I was really embarrassed about the lyrics because it was the first thing I'd written and I just threw them in their faces and ran away.' Fortunately, they were impressed with the lyrics she left them with. So she wrote more and so did her sister. 'The second trip I co-wrote "Success", and wrote a few other little bits and pieces. Kylie and I were going to get together and write, but we didn't have time to see each other, so she wrote a song for me.'

Not that the work took place only in the Bronx. She also did some of the recording in a studio in the downtown Manhattan area of SoHo. This was a less notorious area than the Bronx but it still served up for her plenty of food for thought. 'There's a real up side and a real down side to New York,' she said. 'You see a lot of poverty here that you don't really see in Australia. But most of the time it's up – the city is really busy and you get a lot of energy from that.'

In the process of making her funk album, the girl from

Australia was attempting to live the authentic lifestyle for the music she wanted to make. As well as being aware of the rough parts of America, she was also mindful that it was a difficult market to succeed in for a foreign musical artist. 'To crack it in America you've got … to come over here for a long time to sell and promote your record,' she said. 'But I'm prepared for that – that's what I want to do.' Ever the ambitious hard-worker, she was nonetheless quick to draw a definite distinction between fame and success. 'I don't want to be famous, I just want to be successful in what I do. There's a big difference.'

Elsewhere in her career, she has also spoken openly of her desire to be and remain famous.

Although she had eschewed the temptation of working with Stock Aitken Waterman as her sister had, it remained difficult for her to entirely differentiate herself from her sibling. As she chased musical success, there were inevitable comparisons to be drawn between her and her sister. She was clear from the very start that their styles would be different, no matter what people said or expected. 'I think a large percentage of people will expect it to be like hers [Kylie's music],' she said. 'I never wanted to record the same music as my sister.'

But she conceded that her sister's success was not a hindrance but in fact it could also help, in that it gave her an extra push to succeed herself. 'In some ways that's really good because you're pushing yourself just that much more to make it that much better. The pressure's on a bit but it can be really good – make you work that much harder.'

Not that her choice of sound was ruled only by a desire to differentiate herself from her sister, of course. 'We made a conscious decision not to go with a UK sound,' she said. 'Not to steer clear of what Kylie was doing, but because we wanted a funky black American sound. The first trip I made over there, they had already written the songs. I wrote a rap to go with one of them.'

Pop music is a fickle industry and Dannii was under no illusions about this as she prepared her first album, *Dannii* (rereleased as *Love and Kisses* in Europe). Indeed, she said that her awareness of this simply spurred her to work harder and better. 'I'm never 100 per cent happy with anything I do, which I think is a good attitude because there's always room for improvement,' she said. 'Everyone can love you one day and then hate you the next. It's that flavour-of-the-month thing, so you've just got to be better than before and keep moving on, and I think that's a good thing because you just keep growing as a person.' She was approaching the questions of where to launch her career first with her usual canny eye and fearless attention to detail. 'America is the obvious choice because it's got an American dance feel, and Moody and Bell are big on the American dance scene. The fact it's a bit controversial with them recording me could also attract attention to the song, but it's a risk. There are so many records being released over there. It could easily get lost in the rush,' Dannii said. 'On the other hand, I'm known in England through *Home and Away*, which has 14 million viewers. Those sort of numbers are hard to ignore, but I don't know if people in England will go for American-style music.'

In the final analysis, she was clear that she had to live or die on her own merits. She believed she could not – and in any case did not want to – rely on her sister. 'I don't think I'm guaranteed any free ride to the top because I'm Kylie's sister,' she said as she prepared for the big launch. 'I'm going to make it on my own.'

Her first single was released in February 1990. Called 'Love and Kisses', it entered the Australian charts in March and spent a respectable 15 weeks there, peaking at number four. By April, it had sold some 60,000 copies and achieved gold status in Australia. In September, she released her second single, 'Success'. This was one of the tracks she co-wrote, so she was particularly delighted when it lived up to its title and gave her another Top 40 hit in Australia. Then came a third single 'I Don't Wanna Take This Pain'.

With Dannii building up a head of steam in the Australian charts, it was time to move beyond those shores. In December, Mushroom Records struck a deal with MCA Records to license her music abroad. There were exciting promotional duties to fulfil. For instance, Dannii signed copies of her album at venues such as Sunflower Records at Garden City. As she did so, she reflected again on the fact that music was her real ambition. 'Acting was just a way to pass time while I got the record together, and now that it's finished it will be full steam ahead,' she told an Australian paper.

She had her 19th birthday as she was in the midst of this promotional maelstrom and celebrated in down-to-earth style with a quiet party at the family home in Melbourne with mum Carol, dad Ron and brother Brendan. Kylie was on a flight to Britain and could not be there. Meanwhile, her manager Terry Blamey was plotting how to launch her to ever more fans and nations as a music star. Dannii herself told a reporter that she was not aiming to follow in the footsteps of her sister's pop career, however. 'It will be completely different to Kylie's – more like rock music, for the US,' she said.

By the time she turned 20, Dannii had achieved so much. She was asked to look ahead 20 years and predict what she would have achieved by then. 'I don't know,' she replied. 'I don't really like to look into the future that much. I know there's going to be a lot of good things in store, if I do the right thing. I just keep a very open mind. If tomorrow I decide that I don't like acting and singing and clothes designing and I want to become a pilot, then that's what I do. I've got a whole big life ahead of me, and I don't know, maybe I'll fall in love, and quit it all and have kids. I don't know. I just keep my mind open.'

Her fashion and musical activities meant Dannii was increasingly facing the gentlemen and women of the

Above: Dannii Minogue on *Young Talent Time* in Australia. © *Rex Features*

Below: The cast of the show with, far left on the bottom row, Minogue.

© *Rex Features*

Above: Dannii and Kylie Minogue before all the global domination.

© *Rex Features*

Below left: Young Minogue sisters.

© *Rex Features*

Below right: Minogue and grandmother Millicent Jones.

© *Rex Features*

Above: Home and away
with Craig McLachlan
and Danni Minogue.
© Rex Features

Right: More *Home
and Away*. *© Rex Features*

Minogue and
boyfriend Julian
McMahon.

© Rex Features

Pre-judge days for Minogue and Piers Morgan.

Above: Minogue shared her *Big Breakfast* duties with puppets Zig and Zag.

© *Rex Features*

Below: She's the one that they want – Minogue with dancers from *Grease*.

© *Rex Features*

Above: Flanked by fellow stars of *The Vagina Monologues* Kika Markham and Meera Syal. © *Rex Features*

Below: Dannii Minogue (bottom row, second from left) joined an all-star gala performance of *The Vagina Monologues* at the Albert Hall in April 2002. © *Rex Features*

Minogue and
Jacque Villeneuve.
© *Rex Features*

press for interviews. The media were in love with her and queued up to grab her thoughts. She arrived at many of these interviews bracing herself for the usual questions and comments that connected her with Kylie, but she was pleasantly surprised when she discovered that the press were beginning to view her as her own person. 'I remember I had to do a whole lot of interviews when the first single was released,' she said. 'I thought every journalist would ask about me and Kylie, but none of them did. Each one assumed that the others had asked me about that, so they were all looking for something different.'

Well, she was not about to complain about that. She was relishing her increased success and renewed independence. With both came more fame and recognition. Being recognised while out and about has often been something that Dannii has found amusingly confusing. 'I just kind of walk down the street ... someone will be looking at me and I'll get really upset. It was only yesterday when I was in a coffee shop and this guy was staring at me. I thought, Why is he staring at me like that? Because I just forget. Then I thought, Well, if I was in this coffee shop and some star walked in I'd probably be sitting there staring as well. The thing is, you don't expect to see them walk in.'

She had not always been amused by the fuss; in fact, on some occasions it has actually scared her. She recalls a trip to London's Oxford Street with Kylie at a peak in her sister's fame. 'It was very scary when I went on a trip with Kylie there,' she said. 'She was working and I was travelling around having a holiday. It's very scary stuff, how people react to her. I knew she was big over there, everyone knew her. I didn't realise until I got there – no one over here can understand the impact. It was just berserk.'

Berserk indeed, but at least in those days she was able to spend more time with Kylie. Face time with her sister was becoming an increasingly rare treat for Dannii as both of the sisters were handed ever more hectic schedules full of international travel. 'I hardly ever get to see my sister because she's overseas most of the time and Michael [Hutchence, Kylie's then rock-star boyfriend] is busy working on an album. We don't go out that much because it's pretty difficult being together and being out in public.'

Dannii was keenly aware that she was opening herself up to a hostile hearing from the press. She was not sure how she felt about the potential this gave her for harsh verdicts from the media. 'I don't know,' she said. 'If they rubbish me, if they say I'm jumping on the bandwagon and riding on Kylie's success, they're going to look like fools. I'm doing *Home and Away*, and people can see that's she's not acting for me. Also, the music is completely different to her style. If they do rubbish me – it happened to Kylie – well, I'm not going to get good press all through my career, so it's going to come sometime. I mean, Kylie got rubbished so much, but it didn't stop her career. In one way, it kind of helped. I'm really happy with what I've done. I'll put it out and, if they like it, they like it. If they don't, they don't.'

Dannii already had a multifaceted career, with her fingers in many pies. In truth, we had seen nothing yet and she has added more strings to her bow of late. But there was already enough going on for her back then for her to be asked if she had a favourite path: fashion, music or acting. 'I like all of them,' she laughed, but went on to admit that one day she might feel the need to downsize. 'I want to be able to do all of them as long as I can. If the pressure builds up and I feel I'm sacrificing one or all of them to keep going, then I'll concentrate on fewer things.'

For now, she was most keen to promote her music – primarily to one of the world's biggest audiences. It was hard work for her trying to crack the American music market. It involved painfully lengthy journeys across the United States to knock on the doors of radio stations in the hope they would add her tracks to their playlists. The hours are long, staring out at identical freeways, and, even once you reach a station, the basic mathematics of the situation offer the artist a low probability of success. 'In America, I'm feeding myself to the sharks,' she said. 'Of the programmers you meet, 10 per cent will actually listen to your record and 0.5 per cent might use it on their radio station. On street level, you play the hip clubs. And these people who are nobodies have the power to decide who is going to be a star.'

These were tough challenges and required every bit of

her steely determination and ambition. It is easy for the pop artist on the American trail to feel unappreciated and to become overwhelmed at times by a sense that their efforts are entirely in vain.

Luckily for Dannii, her television work was being recognised with a growing number of awards. She was named the Most Popular Female Television Personality on 9 March 1990 at the Australian television industry's respected Logie Awards. Then at the Sheraton Wentworth Hotel she picked up the Variety Club Young Variety Award. 'I see it as something special, a really big compliment, to get an award for something,' said Dannii. 'But I don't work to receive awards. I just work to make whatever I'm making really good, and then if people like it they like it. If they like it enough to give you an award, that's like a big compliment.'

Honoured as she undoubtedly was, it was overseas where Dannii was hoping for success. When she came to Britain to launch her music, she was somewhat taken aback by the experience. 'When I arrived in the UK, I was completely overwhelmed!' she remembered. 'I was like a kid in Disneyland. There's no way in the world I thought that all these years later I'd still be living here, writing and producing records. I just remember feeling like a country bumpkin and not knowing what was going on at all. People would get excited because I was going on *Blue Peter* and I didn't even know what those shows were. I'd be thinking, What are you talking about? What's a *Blue Peter* badge?! I really had no idea where I was or what I was doing but I didn't care because I was having such a good time.' It turned out to be a much longer visit than she had ever anticipated. 'I actually thought it was going to be a three-week trip to promote the single – I had one suitcase packed and then I was going home,' she said in 2006. 'Sixteen years later I'm still here.'

However, let nobody underestimate what a big step Dannii felt her initial move was. Britain's big cities often have visible Australian populations nowadays, but that does not mean the move is necessarily made lightly. 'I know it's risky travelling at the moment and I'm going to be terribly homesick,' Dannii told the *Herald Sun* on the eve of her departure in 1991. 'The day the Gulf War broke out I just felt ill all day. I couldn't eat because I was so worried about everything. I realise living in Europe is a lot more dangerous than being in Australia, but you have to put things into perspective, the bombing in Downing Street freaked me out. I'll certainly be careful about where I go and what I do. But look at the people in Israel, they try to live as normal a life as possible, despite what's going on around them.'

Her reference to the people of Israel is by no means a random affair but actually part of a healthy interest that Dannii has in Judaism and Jewish culture, marking her out as something of a Philosemite.

Back in the 1990s, though, she freely admitted that it was a 'frightening' time for her as she attempted to gain global recognition for her work. Once more, the Kylie comparison was proving a mixed blessing for Dannii, who was as honest as ever. 'Yes, I was the chubbier sister. Yes, I was the less famous sister. I was everything the papers said I was. But I just knew I had to keep going.'

At times, Dannii has sounded dismissive of Australia, but in truth she has enormous affection for the country, its climate and its people. She was asked later what regrets she had in life, and listed her move to the capital as one of them. 'Since I came to Britain to make a new international career for myself, I've missed the hot Australian weather and all my friends. I regretted having to leave Australia, but the market there isn't big enough. I have to make it happen in Britain and the States.' Of the challenge to becoming a global music star, she said, 'I'm looking forward to it, it will be a challenge for sure. The competition will be different, but you have to go in confident.'

It was a challenge and a memorable one, for Dannii's global promotional push was eventful to say the least, including as it did performances in gay nightclubs, searches by Filipino soldiers, groupies galore and even an encounter with disgraced heavyweight boxer Mike Tyson. It was at the American launch of her album that she met Tyson, who had recently been released from prison. 'A DJ friend of mine called Al Sure invited him along. I didn't even know he was coming until 10 or 12 of the biggest guys you've ever seen, his bodyguards, walked into the nightclub where we were releasing my record *Love and Kisses*,' said Dannii. 'He was very quiet but when he found out I was an Australian he kept telling me how much he loved [retired Australian boxer] Jeff Fenech, and that Jeff Fenech was his hero.'

Some eyebrow-raising moments came in Manila, as she recalled while looking back at the Southeast Asian leg of the jaunt. 'I was shocked when I went to a few of those countries,' said Dannii. 'I never expected the huge military presence everywhere. When I went to one radio station in Manila, there was a sign saying "Leave explosives at the door", and all these soldiers with machine guns checked everyone out. It was very scary.'

Frightening in a different way were her experiences with overdevoted fans in England. She had seen the sort of hysteria that can build around celebrities first-hand during past visits to the capital with Kylie, but nothing could prepare her for some of the excesses of fans. 'It gets a bit scary really, they follow me everywhere I go taking photos even if it means they have to drive up to Birmingham or Manchester to do so,' she said. 'Sometimes there are as many as 12 of them. It makes it really hard to go out on a date or anything.'

Then came the appearances at a gay club in the French capital, another memorable experience for her on the road. 'There is a gay club in Paris that is extreme,' she said. 'Everybody gets very dressed up. It's very theatrical.' She was also offered drugs in Paris but insists that she had also encountered such offers in Melbourne as well.

On and on came the pressure for her to do a duet with

Kylie. The pressure included a huge financial potential, but both Minogue girls were keen to resist that temptation. 'Something like that would probably be very successful but we've worked too hard to establish ourselves as creditable artists by blowing it on such a song,' said Dannii.

After so much promotional touring, Dannii was to return to the country of her birth for a while. When she went back to Australia having spent so much time overseas, she seemed to feel as if she were a daughter returning to her stuffier home having spent time in some more exciting and modern climbs. In no area of her life did she feel this more keenly than in what she chose to wear. Dannii has often enjoyed some racy and edgy looks, but she felt these were harder to pull off comfortably in Australia. 'It's just me, my personality. I love really wild, way-out clothes,' Dannii said. 'In London I can wear wilder things than in Melbourne because there's more fashion happening because of the close proximity to Europe. But they are conservative compared to the US. Australia is conservative in its own way. On the rock scene here, people pretty much do what they want, but, as far as dance and pop go, people have definite opinions about what you should be doing and what you should like. I was wary coming back here because I've done all this stuff overseas that not many people have seen and, if you come back completely different, people do a double-take. It's like, "That wasn't the girl who left a year ago. That's not our Dannii."

'They freak out. I feel that the public treats you almost like a daughter – they all have an opinion.'

Dannii has always been nothing short of frank about how she feels she is perceived. She loves her country of birth but is also realistic about it. Indeed, for Dannii, one can truly say one loves a country only if one is willing to be so honest about it. She was rising above what she saw as the provincialism of her background and becoming known around the world. For the next chapter of her rise to fame she was to return to Australia, though. It was time for Dannii, so many times a star on television, to hit the big screen for the first time.

CHAPTER FOUR

sexy secrets

Dannii is well known for her part in the soap *Home and Away*, but one of her acting projects, which has become forgotten, is her role in the 1992 film *Secrets*. The film has often been compared to *The Breakfast Club*, and it would therefore seem to be *Secrets* that Dannii was referring to when she said in 1991, 'I've been offered a part in a *Breakfast Club*-type Aussie movie but singing is the thing I've always loved, and I'm very grateful I can make a living doing it. I've been very lucky.'

The film was about a group of teenage fans who were caught up in the frenzied excitement surround the 1964 tour of Australia undertaken by the Beatles. She played a teenager besotted with the band – so much so that, when she prayed at her Catholic church, she saw the faces of the Fab Four in front of her at the altar. She and her fellow fans end up locked in the basement of the Southern Cross Hotel. Although the excitement around Dannii has never reached that enjoyed by the Beatles, as we have seen her own experiences with excitable fans did give her a good insight into the part she was playing in *Secrets*. 'I have met fans who have just burst into tears when they saw me,' she said. 'If I go out with friends who aren't in the industry, somebody will come up and ask for my autograph and just be really excited and they're kind of, like, it's only you, what are they so excited about? Sometimes they don't know how to deal with it, or they get annoyed because we're sitting down eating, but I get excited when I meet other people. I mean, I don't ask for their autograph but there is some sort of buzz when you've seen somebody on TV or on the big screen and then you see them in real life.'

Being recognised and recognising, Dannii was familiar with both sides of the fame game and thus naturally equipped for this aspect of her part in *Secrets*.

However, most of her research for the role came not from Dannii's own experiences but from watching footage of the madness that used to surround the Beatles, particularly from their female fans – and, by happy coincidence, she personally encountered one of the Fab Four after making the film. 'You can see into the eyes of those girls – they lived for nothing else than the Beatles. They don't understand the band are real human beings. They think they're godlike. I've had my share of being haunted by single fans, but, as a collective, what

Beatles fans were to the Beatles is a completely different story. Bourke Street in Melbourne was just a sea of people – that wouldn't happen today. After I'd finished the film, I was in New York and Paul McCartney was sitting at the next table from me in a restaurant. In the movie, Didi's favourite Beatle is Paul and so I'd really studied him, and I'm sitting there just blown away, thinking, This guy's just a legend. I mean in the 60s he could never have done that.'

Dannii was absolutely 'stoked' to land the part. 'It was another dream come true,' she told the *Hobart Mercury*, before outlining the slightly unconventional route to getting the part. 'I didn't think I would get the opportunity so soon. I was really stoked that Michael [Pattinson] just asked me to do it – there was no audition. He had more faith in me than I had faith in me to act in a movie. I mean I've never done formal acting training, and, when you're in a soap for so long, the scripts are so limited … you get very blasé about it and people think, if you're a soapie actor, you can't act. I'd sort of got to the point where I thought, Can I do it? But Michael had so much confidence, and I knew he'd worked with actors who hadn't seen a camera before. He'd see somebody walking down the street and think you would be great for this part.'

His laid-back approach to filmmaking was actually enough to fill Dannii with confidence as she took on the part.

For Dannii, this was perhaps a shrewd choice for her

debut big-screen appearance. Rather than go for a big role that would see her under pressure to 'carry' the film, she chose an ensemble part that offered her prominence but little pressure. She had, she claimed, turned down numerous parts before accepting the role in *Secrets*. 'I have an agent in LA and I've been getting scripts over the last year, and hating them all,' she said. 'But this had a great script. It was exciting as an artist, working with great people. Noah Taylor would walk out of the room and his character would walk back in – amazing,' she said. 'There are a lot of giggles and laughs. It is very funny.' She says that her role as Didi, 'a pretty weird, introverted kid', was challenging because 'she's very religious and I'm not religious at all. It was also hard playing a character younger than myself, rather than older.'

Dannii was said by the *Sun* to have received a fee of £220,000 for filming *Secrets*. Not bad for a month's filming work in New Zealand. All the same, at this point she was feeling immense pressure on herself career-wise. 'If I fail now, it's my name, my image, reputation; everything on a worldwide scale will be stamped non-achiever,' she said. 'It's not like opening a corner store and, if it doesn't work, you try again. At 20, I'm looking at the prospect that, if I fail, my life could be f***ed. It's that intense all the time. And the points when you feel it most are when things are going the best.'

Secrets was launched with some impressive gala premieres in Sydney and Melbourne, yet more moments of glamorous pride for Dannii. However, the reviews for *Secrets* were few and often harsh. The *Sunday Herald Sun* was scathing of Dannii by implication when it turned to her during its write-up of the film. 'Then there's Dannii Minogue, proving big sister Kylie's success is based on talent,' wrote its reviewer, who nonetheless pointed the finger elsewhere when it came to the real problem with the film. 'The fault lies in the script: Jan Sardi, one of Australia's more accomplished writers, has written some clever lines, but doesn't know when to yell "cut".'

The *Sunday Mail* was scarcely more positive in its review of the film. 'Teenagers may find something entertaining in this story as the kids talk about love, sex, parents, teachers, families and enemies, but it is all so awkwardly sandwiched with choreographed scenes of them passing the time in the dank basement that most adults will find it an unforgivable waste of otherwise charmingly youthful talent,' it concluded breathlessly.

The *Sydney Morning Herald*'s Lynden Barber wrote, 'Dannii Minogue is a turn-up for the books as an enigmatically taciturn girl.' Of the film overall, Barber was less convinced: 'Despite the performances, however, I was never entirely convinced that these people were inhabitants of the era. *Secrets* suffers from looking very much the 1990s version of the 1960s: well crafted, perhaps, but with something getting lost in the translation.'

The Age's Neil Jillett took a rather similar position.

He concluded that Dannii and her fellow leads 'do well with a thin script' but that the film itself all too quickly fell into 'a series of trite confessions about sex and insecurity'.

The *Courier Mail* was happier with the film, writing, '*Secrets* has been released just in time for the hordes of teenagers on holidays looking for a storyline with a little love, a few laughs and great music.'

Like many publications, the South African *Sunday Mail* compared the film to *The Breakfast Club* and wrote 'enjoyable holiday viewing'.

At least the *Sun Herald* had some kinder words about the film to throw into the critical mix. Its review said, 'Though it gets off to an excellent start, the movie, like its characters, quickly gets locked into a situation which tends to slow things down to a crawl.' All the same, the review concluded that *Secrets* was 'above average'. Elsewhere in the same newspaper, Dannii was profiled and the article praised her for her low-pressure choice of debut film and described *Secrets* as 'a delightful ensemble comedy'. Which was more than had been said about Kylie's cinematic debut when she had appeared in the 1989 film *The Delinquents*, a tale of a forbidden love.

As Dannii released *Secrets*, she rather appropriately gave an interview in which she revealed many personal details. Asked who would be her ideal dining companion, she said, 'Michael Jackson, because nobody knows what he's really like. I'd love to discover the truth. Rowan Atkinson has a great sense of humour and I'd also love to meet French actor Jean-Marc Barr. who starred in *The Big Blue*. He's the most desirable man I've ever seen.'

She continued with the chat, speaking about her ever-developing sense of fashion. 'I like sexy catsuits and dresses by Plein Sud, tight Pucci pants, casual clothes from Whistles and the Changing Room,' she said. 'I'm a chameleon with clothes, I can slop around in ripped jeans, wear straight suits or something radical and bizarre. I buy bits and pieces all over the world. I've just come back from New York, where I bought a long black Patricia Field PVC ball gown and silver leather chaps. In London I go to Hyper Hyper one day, Browns the next. Outrageous clothes are hard to find. I adore black bras and black see-through shirts or black PVC shorts teamed with a silver chain-mail vest, which I bought in New York for £1,000. It's beautiful. Kylie and I never swapped clothes, even when we were teenagers, because we're both such different shapes. I'm much more voluptuous, and we like different things.

'I've got shoes from all over the world and they're the biggest pain in the neck to pack. Kylie bought me a great pair of Katharine Hamnett football boots with heels. I need to wear heels because I'm only 5 foot 1 inch tall, but I'm still 2 inches taller than her.' She readily admitted that she can take a long time to get ready before a night out. 'It depends on whether I wash my hair or not. If I do, it takes three hours because it's very long and thick. If not, about an hour. I shower, then go through my wardrobe, changing my mind about ten times before deciding what to wear. My makeup is as varied as the rest of my stuff: I have a little bit of this, a little bit of that. My base is by Guerlain and my powder by Lancome. I use Chanel eye shadow because I like their colours best and Japanese lipsticks by Kanebo because they stay on best. I love very rich colour on my lips and I think because the Japanese traditionally used red lipsticks in their drama that they have developed the best scarlets with staying power.'

Dannii had continued to plough a musical path as well. In 1992, she released a reissue of her debut album. It was called *Love and Kisses*, and it included remixes and dance versions of songs from her debut album. The previous year, a Steve 'Silk' Hurley remix of 'Baby Love' had given the UK market a hint of what was to come. The single reached number 14 in the British charts and the reissued album edition sold 60,000 copies here. She then released a cover of the Jackson Five song 'Show You the Way to Go'. The song was later included on a charity album to raise money for the British Spastics Society. With her musical career developing, Dannii flew to Turkey to sing at the Cesme Festival.

But her single 'Love's on Every Corner' performed very disappointingly – and was not even released in Australia – and then she was voted worst female singer in a magazine poll in early 1993.

She then got involved in an onscreen bust-up with presenter Mark Lamarr on Channel 4's late-night show *The Word*. Lamarr was mocking her musical career, so Dannii emptied a jug of water over him. It made for great television and won her numerous admirers. 'It's not that I hate him now, it just like "You were a tw*t, you said something that pi**ed me off and I threw water on your head." Big deal, end of story, done,' she said during a subsequent interview with gay magazine *Attitude*. 'It must have been embarrassing for him because he brought me on the show just to take the p**s out of me. Like "I'm Mark Lamarr I'm really cool because I think Dannii really sucks." I hate that style of comedy.'

When she turned up to perform at the Christmas show of a London radio station, she was booed by the 5,000-strong crowd. At Wembley she had been booed by teenage fans, who chanted, 'We hate Dannii' and 'Lose some weight.' She was visibly upset and rushed from the stage. When the entire ensemble reappeared on the stage to perform the evening's finale together, Dannii stood shyly at the back, wounded by her previous experience. 'It was embarrassing,' recalled an onlooker. 'The fans turned against her and ridiculed her.'

This was long before the era of *Heat* and the predominance of 'size zero' celebrities, but even then females were sitting targets for jibes if they were anything other than thin. With her weight increasing, she was increasingly the subject of unflattering press photographs. Snappers would wait outside events she was due at and capture images of her stepping out of a car, and all too often they would publish the ones that made her thighs seem widest. 'She's a vegan,' a spokesperson for her felt compelled to explain to the press, even though she was clearly not overweight. 'You should see her in the flesh. It's just that she's not as skinny as Kylie.'

There was more abuse in store for her when she attended a Michael Jackson concert in London. It was the opening night of the pop legend's tour. As Dannii relaxed in the hospitality tent in Wembley, she was verbally attacked by two thugs who had managed to find their way through the security cordon. 'Get your tits out,' one of them shouted. His companion was more menacing, shouting, 'I'm going to chin that stuck-up bitch.' They were eventually dragged away, but Dannii was left shaken.

Things were sometimes scarcely better for her in America at this point. Dannii was keen to crack the Stateside market but was getting something of a cold shoulder in some quarters despite her efforts in the opening months of 1992. Hollywood gossip columnist Michael Musto went as far as openly mocking her and her attempts to raise her profile in America. 'I get no fewer than four calls from a publicist who's promoting Dannii Minogue, the singing sister of Brit (!) pop chanteuse Kylie Minogue and a "big star in England" (so's my mother),' he wrote cattily. 'Too bad I've met Dannii who was bland, that I've seen her perform (blander) and that I'm not even interested in Kylie, let alone her sibs.'

However, she had also been receiving a number of honours and awards from her fans around the world. In the autumn of 1991, she received nominations in multiple categories of the annual *Smash Hits* magazine awards. The pop magazine's readers voted Dannii Best New Artist, and she finished second (to Madonna) in the Most Fanciable Female and Best Female Singer in the World categories. Her debut album was also nominated in the category of Album of the Year. Encouraging signs for her and just two months later the readers of UK *Big* magazine voted her no less than the World's Best Female Pop Star. She would soon become more accustomed to such exciting honours, the likes of which she continues to receive to this day.

With such accolades, Dannii emerged surprisingly unscarred and still confident of her abilities, despite her often cruel media treatment in England. 'I think, for a while there, everyone expected a certain kind of hit song and, when they didn't get exactly what they were looking for, they turned on me,' she said. 'You can't always be at the top, this whole thing is like a roller coaster but you've got to keep trying. I've decided that, this time while it's up there, I'm going to grab it and not let it go. For a while, I thought that, if it didn't happen now (with the new album), that I was going to pack it all in. But I've confirmed to myself that I do have what it takes and that people do like me. I want hit songs and

I want to be at the top of the charts. If these sorts of songs are what people want me to do, then I'm happy to do it.' She denied that she was in any way compromising herself. 'It's only a compromise when I lose my audience – and I don't want to do that.'

Why, she was asked frequently, did she do so much better outside Australia than inside? 'It's something to do with the population of each country,' she replied. 'There are a million different politics involved. One is that Australian radio doesn't really support dance and pop music as much as it does in the UK. There is an extra hysteria in England that you will never get in Australia. They get very obsessed and very frantic about people, whereas Australians are much more laid back.'

She released her second album in the autumn of 1993 called *Get Into You*. Although it was not a summer release, Dannii nonetheless had aimed for a bright and breezy effect with the album. 'With this album, I just set out to make something that's happy, that's fun and something that you can bop around to,' she said. 'When I first recorded *Love and Kisses*, it was very American, then we remixed it for the English market by making it more poppy and funky – that worked well so we headed along those lines again. Recording this was a long process and there were a lot of lonely times in lonely places where I didn't know anyone and I thought I couldn't wait for it to be over. But now I've got a piece of work that I think, Wow – I really like it.'

Amid all this media fuss and career efforts, Dannii had the usual hopes and desires in her private life that all women do, but feared that the chances of her finding true love were slim, to say the least. 'I was in Australia and I told my mum I should probably become a nun,' she recalled. Dannii had briefly dated 2 Unlimited rapper Ray Slijngaard in the early 1990s but she had not, as yet, been lucky in love. Indeed, she had recently become so career-focused that she was feeling increasingly isolated. 'I spend all day every day working towards being famous,' she said. 'The most exciting part of my day is coming back to my hotel and finding a fax waiting for me from a friend who is far away. I'm so distant from all the people I care about.' So who would have thought that not just true love, but also marriage, were just around the corner for our heroine?

Dannii first met actor Julian McMahon in 1991, while she was working on *Home and Away*. Within a few years, they would become an item and her siblings were delighted for her that she had seemingly found her man. Her normally shy brother Brendan said that Julian 'has made [Dannii] happy, I think they are fantastic together.'

When Kylie was asked whether the couple would last, she laughed and said, 'That's like asking if I believe in Santa Claus,' but she also added more seriously, 'I hope it lasts.'

The press noted that with her new look and new man

Dannii was proving the doubters wrong. 'They aren't laughing at Dannii Minogue now,' said the *Sunday Tasmanian*. 'The fashion-victim snipes have withered. The bitchy comparisons with big sister Kylie are few and far between.'

So who was this new man who was causing such a rethink in how Dannii was perceived by both press and family and friends?

Julian McMahon was born in 1968, the second of three children born to William McMahon and his wife Sonia. They were a power couple: William was a politician who went on to become the Australian Prime Minister and then Sir William, while Sonia was a glamorous socialite. His father was already 61 years of age when Julian was born, but the family was a reasonably close and loving one. A chauffeur reportedly drove him to Sydney Grammar School each day – though he has claimed he took the train for a three-stop journey – where he became a prefect. Happy times; indeed, Julian once recalled, 'The only traumatic thing about my childhood was when my mother took away my teddy bear.' Describing the neighbourhood he and his two siblings grew up in he said, 'We rode our bikes around. Walked to the pub. It was all so accessible. You felt like everybody was your mate.'

Young Julian was served an early taste of fame when, at just three years of age, he captured the nation's heart by banging on a toy drum in front of the media the day his father became Prime Minister. The toddler was seemingly destined for a public life and so it turned out, as he left law school in favour of a successful career in modelling. He went on to appear in shows in Europe and America, and also starred in a commercial for jeans giants Levi Strauss.

He then turned to acting and landed a part on Dannii's soap *Home and Away*, in which he played a soldier. This was the turn of fate that brought them together, and, by the time he appeared in promotional videos for two of Dannii's singles, they were a couple. They had known each other for a while before, but, as Dannii explained, some 'explosive chemistry' suddenly erupted between them at a Sydney awards ceremony. They then moved from friendly colleagues to a romantic item who were engaged and quickly on the road to getting hitched.

The Minogue clan could hardly have been happier for them and Dannii's friends were impressed, with one of them describing the pairing as 'one of the most glamorous things in the world' – but not everyone was overjoyed by this budding relationship. McMahon's family were reported to be less than impressed by the new bonding in some instances. But, whatever the truth of the reports, the couple were determined to go ahead. As both of them were famous figures, they sold the rights to the event to *Woman's Day* magazine in Australia and *Hello!* magazine in the UK. Their fee was reported to be $100,000, which was a fortune for such a deal in those days. For instance, when Donald

Trump wedded Marla Marples, they reportedly received just $30,000. The press clearly considered the couple a hot ticket, as just a few months prior to the wedding they had been paid by *Hello!* magazine to be photographed during a holiday in the Caribbean. A UK security expert was hired to ensure privacy for the event. 'It's a closed shop and it's going to be virtually impossible for anyone to get near it,' said Nicole Miller, who handled the international sales of the wedding snaps.

Dannii was straightforward in her verdict as to why the price had been set so high. 'I guess,' she mused, 'I guess when two famous people get together it's something to talk about.'

She also felt that celebrity romance stories bring some sunshine into the lives of people in increasingly dark and difficult times. 'People really want to hear about the bride thing and, while I'm in the country, I'm happy to talk about it because there are problems with the economy and the world and there's so much unhappiness,' she said during a promotional visit to Australia. 'I thought, Let's give people some happy news and let's talk about it. I'm feeling good and I want to share it. The majority of people in Australia want to know about it because, hey, Kylie and I are joe-blows who started off when no one knew who we were and they've watched us grow for years.'

Dannii was looking forward to it and told an interviewer that Brendan would be one of the groomsmen, while Kylie would be bridesmaid. 'And Dad will be walking me down the aisle,' she said proudly. 'The wedding dress is a secret. I can tell you Kylie is helping me with the dress design and I'm designing the bridesmaids' dresses, which will be beautiful,' she added with a smile.

The marriage took place in January 1994 at the Grand Hyatt Hotel in Melbourne in front of 250 guests. Apart from the magazine deal, the media were banned from the ceremony, and when an English journalist was found staying at the hotel he was reportedly asked to leave.

Among those on the guest list were Mushroom Records boss Michael Gudinski, performer Ronnie Burns and Beven Addinsall, Dannii's former *Young Talent Time* co-star, as well as the American actress Lois Larimore, who was McMahon's onscreen wife in his latest television drama. On the night, Julian's mother, Lady McMahon, wearing a bright-green evening dress, was the last of the 250 guests to arrive, having opted to stay elsewhere.

Fans surrounded the hotel hoping for a glimpse of the happy couple. As some of the neck-craning onlookers admitted, they were also hopeful of a sighting of Kylie. Two teenage fans even checked into the expensive hotel in the hope of seeing Kylie. Their plan was to spend most of their stay travelling up and down in the hotel lifts in the hope that they might share a ride with Kylie. They had saved up for months using the money one of them earned at McDonald's. It is not known if their lift journey wish came true, though the chances seem on the slender side.

At the reception Dannii and Kylie sang together in public for the first time since the *Young Talent Time* era. They joined arms and sang 'We Are Family' together. It was a brilliant highly moving performance. In his speech Julian was moved to tears, prompting some moist eyes in the audience, too, when he said of Dannii, 'She is my world.'

It had been a wonderful night for Dannii, who was truly touched and moved by her new husband's words.

But Mushroom Records chairman Michael Gudinski had a different take on the proceedings. 'God, was I there,' he said candidly. 'It was one of the weirdest weddings I'd ever been to. It was one of the first bits of Australian aristocracy and it was ugly. It had failure written all over it.'

The fantastical experience of the wedding day soon gave way to the reality of married life itself. How would they fare? Some had their doubts from the start. In the run-up to the wedding, Dannii herself had foreshadowed how married life was going to bring important changes for her, as well as touching on the sort of difficulties that the marriage might face geographically. 'Just the marriage is going to be a real change because I've always put career first and now I'm going to put that on hold for a few months and spend time with Julian,' she said. 'Eventually, we'll have kids but it's hard because my family is in Melbourne, my sister lives in London, we live in New York and I work mostly in London, so where does a baby fit in? It's not the kind of thing I can put on the luggage cart on the plane.'

These were not words that oozed confidence, and, if she was feeling less than hopeful, then she was right to do so.

From the start, some sections of the media lined up to take a swipe at her and Julian. She was less than pleased when she learned that the Melbourne newspaper *Sunday Age* had named her and Julian as 'a couple from hell'. The accompanying text asked, 'What do either of them actually do?' This was a peculiar line of attack to say the least. Of all the things one can throw at Dannii, a lack of effort and activity is certainly not one of them.

After a short break from her career to enjoy the beginning of married life, she was soon back and working hard. Soon after her marriage, she was earmarked to stand in for Gaby Roslin on Channel 4's popular morning show *The Big Breakfast*. This was a great gig for her to land. It raised her profile once again and even the antisocial hours that were involved were not a problem, as she explained. 'I'm working my career so we can be together,' said Dannii. 'Getting up early will be easy, because Julian has to be out of bed at 5.30 for filming, so I'm used to getting up with him. I suppose it shows how much in love I am. I'll be going to bed early as well because I'll be working very hard.' However, once the cover slot was over, she was unsure whether she would want to repeat the experience. She was asked during an interview whether she found it easy to be so lively at 6am. 'Yes, but I wouldn't want to be on *The Big Breakfast* every day,' she said. 'I don't like doing just one thing and a breakfast show means I'd have to give up other aspects of my career such as my singing, my fashion and other TV shows.'

No aspects of her career – however successful – could paper over the cracks that were appearing in Dannii's marriage. It seemed she and Julian had been struggling to make their relationship work for some agonising months before it finally came to its unhappy end. On that terrible day, Julian sat her down in his New York apartment and told his wife that it was all over. For Dannii this was a devastating day full of shock, heartbreak and painful disappointment. 'I was 23 and in love,' she said. 'We had a fun time together. We laughed. He was famous, too. Our thing was escaping that and just being together – going to the cinema, going to the beach. If you marry someone and you're in love with them and expecting to be with them for the rest of your life, it is difficult when it ends. I was absolutely devastated. The shock was so consuming. There is always going to be a part of the relationship there. You get over it, but it's a part of your life.'

For Dannii who is ever the perfectionist and one who is perfectly capable of quite intense self-reflection, these were soul-searching days. Her initial verdict was clear, but as to the wider issues she continued to wonder. 'It was a failure in my eyes. It didn't work and I really thought it would work. I constantly analyse it: Why didn't it work out? Why did it go wrong?'

There were suspicions that Dannii had concentrated too much on her career to the detriment of her marriage. While there is no doubt that Dannii is a workaholic and is almost ruthlessly focused on her career, such a commentary would be simplistic and – as she pointed out – unbalanced. 'I've always been career-driven – that didn't change when we got married – but so was he,' she said. 'I was totally focused on our relationship, devoted to our marriage.'

Dannii's professional success is clearly important to her life, and McMahon must have entered the marriage aware of that fact. The awful truth was that it just had not worked out – and for Dannii this truth was painfully hard to take. It took a palpable emotional and physical toll on the young woman. 'When it didn't work, there was a huge hole,' she said. 'I found it hard to eat and hard to sleep – that went on for a very long time. I was skeletally thin. I couldn't see it at the time because I was so stressed. I wasn't trying to be thin but my nerves, that energy, wasted me away. I know he wouldn't have wished that upon me, it's just what I had to go through.' She felt she had to put a front on in public, but, for all the forced smiles, nobody could deny that she was shedding pounds at a highly alarming rate. 'Part of it is, if I can kid myself, I can kid everyone, but it showed. I remember my clothes just falling off me. Magazines said I had anorexia and I looked like a skeleton. I thought,

You're probably right, but it's not helpful. Part of me wanted to go into hibernation, but it was all so public.'

Rumours had it that McMahon's friendship with actress Crystal Atkins was behind the split. Dannii was keen to insist that this was not the cause, but she did admit that she was not expecting the break-up when it happened. 'It was a complete shock and very traumatic,' she said in her first public statement after it. 'It was nothing to do with girls or outside people,' she says. 'It's over. People can like it, lump it, or wrap their chips in it, I don't care. I'm on with my life now.'

The cruel irony for Dannii was that her relatively happy life to date – including growing up in a happy family household with loving parents – made this heartbreak when it came all the harder to deal with. 'The hardest thing for me was losing my naïve take on the world,' she said. 'It was the first tragedy I'd had to deal with. A lot of my friends at school had parents who were breaking up or beating up each other – tragedies they'd had to deal with as children. I never had that. I had a happy childhood and this was reality. It was a shock. It was my dreams broken.'

Although she had plenty of loving people in her life who were only too happy to drop everything to come and support her, Dannii actually preferred to not see them at first. She disappeared into herself and spent long periods in solitude, simply trying to make sense of what had happened to her. 'Afterwards, I spent a lot of time on my own,' she admitted. 'I didn't really see friends that much. I wanted to be on my own to try to understand it. I'm sometimes too strong for my own good and don't like to burden my family and friends. I became very internal.'

Even as she looked back some time later, Dannii's continued sense of despair could not be hidden. 'It still upsets me, absolutely,' she said. 'I won't deny it. It upsets me because it was so important to me. I was in love, that was why I got married. For the first year after we split I was running on empty, but I didn't know it then.' Dannii is a tough character and that steeliness kicked in after a while. 'My work kept me going – even though it was difficult to get up and work. I didn't want the split to destroy my life. You have to make a decision: you can blame everything for the rest of your life on one thing, or you can get up, get on and say, "I'm not going to let this ruin everything." Yes, it is awful, yes, it is tragic, yes, I am going to cry for a million nights in a row. But will I let it take away everything else that's good? No.'

While the renewed strength that Dannii was feeling was a positive, the danger was that finding that strength might mean she would become too tough and somehow close herself off from the chance of future happiness. Dannii was only too aware of this perilous potential. 'The saddest thing is that my view of what love is has changed,' she said. 'He was the person I was going to spend the rest of my life with. I'll never look at someone like that again. It's not that I'm not going to fall in love, it's just that I'm not going to think, We're going to be together for ever. What is "for ever"? I don't know. That got stolen from me, it's shattered. I don't know what "for ever" means.'

This was a jaded, hurt and bewildered young woman speaking. She was not keen to ever open herself to being hurt that way ever again. But this is not an uncommon phase for the recently heartbroken to go through, and in time she would open herself to the possibility again. Yes, she would be hurt again in the future. Eventually, though, she would find more happiness than she would ever have believed to be possible.

In the meantime, she was going through the classic behaviour patterns of a young woman who had been heartbroken. Whether one is famous or not, many of the same rules apply at these times. However, for Dannii, she was about to do one thing that only a famous and beautiful woman could do. Even given that fact, nobody would have predicted her next move.

To understand just how surprising it was, we must briefly return to 1990, when Dannii granted an in-depth interview and photoshoot to the *Sunday Mail* of Queensland. It was during the preparation for the photoshoot that an exchange occurred that subsequently took on a more interesting significance. Dannii's wardrobe assistant was tossing around ideas for the photoshoot: 'And I thought, you know, using these big feathers, topless ... and then this fabric, like this, you know, like Marilyn Monroe, holding it across her chest, with a black bra underneath ...'

At the mention of these more raunchy photographic concepts, Dannii's press officer interrupted: 'Hang on. Nothing too raunchy. Remember this is Dannii Minogue.'

In October 1995, as she licked her wounds over the split with McMahon, Dannii would do a photoshoot that was far more raunchy than anything suggested by her wardrobe assistant back in 1990.

Playboy magazine is an iconic title and a name synonymous with saucy photography of beautiful women. It was founded in the 1950s by Hugh Hefner. Most of the time the women featured in its pages are unknowns who become famous as a result of their *Playboy* photoshoot. However, already famous women have sometimes chosen to strip for *Playboy*. The list is long and includes Daryl Hannah, Kate Fischer, Kim Basinger, Drew Barrymore and Elle Macpherson. The Australian edition of *Playboy* was launched in the late 1970s and it was on the pages of this title that nude photographs of Dannii were featured in 1995. Naturally, she was very flattered. 'I saw it as a compliment when they asked me,' she said. Dannii denied that in participating in the shoot she was acting in any sort of un-sisterly way. 'People say it's trampling women but it's not,' she insisted.

Naturally, posing nude for a high-circulation magazine was a massive decision for Dannii to take. She was surrounded by people who counselled her not to do it, and Dannii listened carefully to their advice. 'Friends said I'd look back and regret it,' she recalled. Their advice was as nothing compared with the reaction of her parents when they heard what she was considering. 'My dad nearly had a heart attack. But I just felt it was real freedom. I was doing my own thing. Doing something shocking. I didn't care what Julian thought. I didn't tell him until afterwards and he still hasn't seen the pictures.' So in this decision she was expressing – in a rather extreme and public way – her freedom from McMahon. 'Most women go to the hairdressers – I did *Playboy*,' she said memorably. 'I chose the photographer, the location, what I did or didn't want to wear and everything else about the pictures. I found it a really liberating, empowering experience.' As well as this motivation, she said, she was also just enjoying a light-hearted experience during such a dark and depressing time. 'It was an act of rebellion in one way, but mostly me having a laugh,' she says. 'Julian went nuts.'

One can only wonder what McMahon must have felt when he first saw the *Playboy* photographs of Dannii, but Lady McMahon was said to be appalled, and, given her reported objections to the marriage, it is easy to imagine her horror.

Dannii had been paid the princely sum of $100,000 for the shoot, and, in subsequent statements, she has been more honest about another of her motivations – the financial one. 'In the end I guess it did lift me up but the reason I did it wasn't to stick two fingers up at Julian at all,' she said. 'At the point that we divorced I was

£150,000 in debt. I had worked my whole entire life. I had earned a lot of money over a long period of time. To be that in debt when you cannot pay your rent, on top of the devastation of the marriage not working out when I really thought it was going to. I loved this person.'

And, since admitting that enormous debt was her major motivation, Dannii has felt rather liberated. 'Ever since then until now, it felt like this dark secret as to why I did *Playboy*. Everybody wagged the finger and said, "What a stupid thing to do!" Because I never ever wanted to admit the trouble I was in and I never wanted anyone to think badly of Julian. I should have been looking at the finances more. I got in big, big trouble. It is kind of nice now to say, "OK, it did look like the most stupid thing to do," but I had no choice and I would never, never ask my family for money. I remember having the contract there and my parents there. My parents did not want me to do this. My dad was standing there saying, "When you do this, that's for ever. You can never, ever change that." I said, "Dad, I don't have any other choice." I signed the bottom of the contract.'

She stressed that she was totally in control of the shoot in all senses. '*Playboy* gave me freedom of choice on everything – when, where, and how. We shot the pictures in the middle of the Nevada Desert, so no one could spy on me. It really was an amazing experience. I wasn't nervous at all and being nude was quite liberating.'

On many occasions when speaking about the *Playboy* shoot – and she is often asked about it, so there are plenty such conversations to draw from – Dannii has emphasised that she felt liberated by it, a word that keeps coming up. 'Thankfully, the upside was it actually was fun and I did feel liberated by it,' she said. 'At the end it probably kind of dug me out of a hole not just financially but … I did get a bit of self-esteem back. I thought, How could I have been so stupid? In every respect! How could I have not seen this coming? Everybody else could see it. How could I let everything turn into this when I should know better. I have worked hard all my life.'

In an ITV chat with Piers Morgan, she insisted she does not look back with regret. 'No I don't. I don't, but I feel more relieved now that people know why I did it. And I looked at the pictures and I thought, Damn, I look all right! The magazine came out and it was the biggest-selling *Playboy* they had ever, ever had. They had to reprint. The biggest compliment was that girlfriends of mine had gone out to buy it, to see what it was all about. They realised they were very tasteful shots and they called me up and said, "You know what? You look beautiful." Then it felt like a celebration of me, only at that point.'

Indeed, when she later posed in her underwear range for the Choice catalogue in 1996, she found that more nerve-racking than she had posing nude for *Playboy*. 'I was kind of nervous posing in the underwear – more nervous than my *Playboy* experience, but the photographer did lots of Polaroids so I could check how I looked. And of course it's important that the clothes look good in a catalogue.'

Last word on the *Playboy* episode concerns the verdict that she might not have expected but welcomed warmly. 'Even my grandma told me I looked beautiful when she saw it,' she says of the shoot.

In the wake of the split, she had a few changes of look, including going for honey-blonde hair colouring. She was dismissive when asked by the *Daily Mirror* whether she was going for the new look because of the split or to try to differentiate herself from her famous sister. 'People try to imply there is some deep psychological reason behind my change of image,' she said. 'That it's because I want to look like Kylie or be different to Kylie. They don't accept that I went to the hairdresser like any other woman and said, "Can I have some streaks"'.

She was often annoyed and exasperated when interviewers asked her about her regularly changing look. To Dannii, this was a non-story and there was nothing strange about it at all. 'Anyone who looks back at their photo album has changed a lot, haven't they?'

In time, the pain and anger began to subside. She was asked about single life and she seemed less chippy and more saddened. 'I learned a lot being married. It's nice to have someone to share things with. But I wouldn't be with anyone for the sake of it. The one I'm looking for will take me away and capture my heart.'

A few months later, she showed little enthusiasm for discussing the split. When asked about it she replied rather evasively. 'Yeah, some of my girlfriends say how they cannot wait to get married, and I say to them, "But you haven't even got a boyfriend yet",' she said.

McMahon remarried, to *Baywatch* actress Brooke Burns, with whom he had a daughter called Madison, but that marriage lasted only a few years.

Ultimately, Dannii looks back at her own failed marriage to McMahon with understandable regret. 'My divorce has been my biggest regret and biggest downfall,' she said. 'It's a scar that I walk around with, because I messed it up. But a lot of time has passed since, and, though Julian and I didn't talk for a few years, I called him a few months ago when I was last in Los Angeles.'

As the scars have healed, she has followed his career. He is now best known for his part on the cosmetic-surgery drama *Nip/Tuck* and in 2004 Dannii caught a few episodes of the hit show, as she explained to *Glamour* magazine. 'I've just seen an episode of *Nip/Tuck*,' she said. 'My friends are addicted to it and they encouraged me to watch. I said, "He's always naked in it, isn't he?" They're like, "Yeah, it's great." That felt weird, but I turned in and thought it was very funny.'

Fortunately, the *Playboy* shoot did nothing to derail Dannii's career, and within weeks of the magazine's hitting the streets she was part of a ChildLine charity single. The song was a Christmas tune and she contributed guest vocals along with other pop acts including boy bands East 17 and Boyzone, as well as fellow Aussie Peter Andre.

Kylie had done her best to support Dannii in her decision to pose for *Playboy* and the two sisters were remaining close and encouraging to each other – which was just as well because soon Dannii would have to be the supportive sister as Kylie faced a personal and very public tragedy. In November 1997, Kylie was woken at 4am by the sound of the telephone ringing. She rubbed her eyes and lifted the receiver. Like many people who receive a call at such a time, she already had the feeling it was bad news. She was told that Michael Hutchence – her former boyfriend – had died in a hotel room. He had drugs and drink in his system but the death appeared to be the result of an act of autoeroticism gone badly wrong. This was the first time in Kylie's life that somebody she had truly loved had died. So it is little wonder that, as a friend revealed, she 'felt her world had crumbled under her feet'. Kylie attended his funeral in Sydney, where she was a largely stoic presence, keen to support his family and friends with their grieving. She has largely retained that position publicly at least and was supported through her own shock and mourning by those closest to her, including Dannii. When a newspaper interviewer tentatively raised the subject of her ex-boyfriend's passing away, she told him she was happy to discuss the matter but insisted that it be made clear that she had not cried while doing so.

Hutchence had been the man who made Kylie grow up. Right from their first meeting, he had left her stunned. 'I was so young really, about 19 or 20,' she recalled. 'Michael sort of stumbled by and I think his first words to me were, "I don't know what we should do first – have lunch or have sex." That was entirely shocking to me – then. I couldn't make any words come out of my mouth, I was too taken aback,' she said.

Like many younger sisters, Dannii watched her big sister go through the rites of passage of life and drew her own lessons from them. Hutchence had joked that his role in life was to 'corrupt Kylie', but she denied he did so in any serious way. 'He wasn't as bad as everyone thought and I wasn't as good,' she said. 'We met somewhere in the middle.' She seemed very well equipped to deal with the grief of his passing, a characteristic that has since been notable in her little sister, who has faced some painful tribulations of her own.

Both of the sisters' stoicism in the face of adversity was to be seen again in the following decade when Kylie was confronted with a life-threatening illness. The support Dannii had given her big sister in the wake of Hutchence's death was to be dwarfed by the challenge facing her in 2005. For now, though, these ever close and loving sisters were unaware of what fate had in store for Kylie. As for Dannii, there was a new love on the horizon.

Could she finally find the happiness that had for so long eluded her and break what was becoming known as the 'curse of the Minogue girls'?

the right formula

Dannii had taken on a number of television presenting duties during the summer of 1995, including *Eggs on Legs*, a regional roadshow spin-off from *The Big Breakfast*, which she presented alongside Richard Orford. It saw her put on a full-on 'wacky' persona to fulfil the brief, and the skits she and Orford performed had names like 'Cock-a-Doodle Do It' and 'Pull the Plug'. It required an early start: she and her co-host rose at 4.30am each day. Orford admitted that he needed three alarm clocks going off to drag himself out of bed in the morning, but for Dannii the early start was less of a challenge. 'Because I'm always travelling through different time zones, funny hours don't bother me,' she said. 'When my alarm goes off, I rush right past the mirror without looking in it and leap in the shower. We rehearse for ages before the show goes on air, so it's easy to look lively and interested.' She ate three breakfasts during each broadcast, 'but I burn it off with all the running around I have to do'.

In the wake of her split from McMahon, she repeated the stint the following summer with Orford once more at her side and a puppet character called Egg White. He spoke of his wonderment at the fact he was working with her. 'We had a lot of fun doing last year's roadshow, so I'm looking forward to all the laughs this year,' he said ahead of the second summer of the show.

They kicked off the second summer in Glasgow, where more than 4,000 fans had turned up to squeal with joy at the fun, which included Dannii taking on an assault course that included her leaping over huge tyres. 'The crowd was sensational – it was better than anything last year,' she said. 'It's a brilliant start to the tour.'

Between the two *Eggs on Legs* tours, Dannii had completed a 16-week stint on the Saturday-morning children's show *It's Not Just Saturday* on STV, which was a mix of fashion, pop, advice and entertainment gossip. She arrived fresh from a holiday in Thailand to record the show in STV's Glasgow studio with co-presenter Gareth Jones. She made a good job of it and the show had an audience that often peaked in excess of 1.5 million, but she faced hostility from one nationalistic Scot. M McEwan of Dundee wrote to the *Daily Record* to ask, 'Why on earth do we need an Australian like Dannii Minogue to come over here and get a job as a presenter on Scottish Television?'

Months later, she appeared on a children's television show called *Scoop*, alongside fellow presenter Sally Gray. 'Dannii is very sweet and she looks great. I'm a big fan of hers,' said Sally.

They had jetted around the world to gather the stories for the show, and this was harder work than it appeared according to *Scoop*'s producer. 'It's not been easy for them,' said Patrick Titley. 'Both Dannii and Sally have been put through their paces and they've done a great job.'

Soon she was presenting more television shows, including magazine show *Electric Circus*. The *Sunday Mail* praised the presenting efforts there of 'the delectable Dannii Minogue'.

Off the back of this renewed profile, she launched a Dannii calendar in the UK. It was a huge hit and sold more than 35,000 copies in its first months on sale. Indeed, in the first week on sale it sold more copies at HMV than the nearest seller – Oasis – had managed in the previous month. Very much on a roll, she fronted ITV's Children Television Awards and also hosted *Top of the Pops* for two successive weeks in 1997. She was given a lucrative commercial gig when she endorsed the relaunch of the Diet Pepsi brand, which saw her as just the ticket in its quest to catch up with its Coca-Cola competitors. These were great times for her as she managed to put the failure of her marriage to McMahon behind her.

However, Dannii was less happy when the media

began to speculate on the size of her chest. One journalist wrote in the *Mirror* newspaper that her bosom had begun to stand out 'like a relief map of North Wales'. The speculation had been fired in January 1996, when Dannii was reportedly sighted at the surgery of a New York man who specialised in boob jobs. News stories suggested that she had spent upwards of £3,000 to increase her bosom size from 34B to 34D. 'I don't read those articles,' Dannii said. 'If you read all the crap, you would give up.' When an interviewer broached the subject with Dannii, she looked at her publicist – who emitted a disapproving 'tut' – and said, 'I'm not answering questions about that.' She did, though, add, 'They've said I am an anorexic, a bulimic … I won't lower myself talking about such things.'

Years later, however, she was more comfortable discussing this. When Piers Morgan asked her about the story during an ITV interview, she cupped her breasts and said with a cheeky smile, 'They're good, aren't they?'

The cost of fame was continuing to confront Dannii. Some kids who lived near her took to ringing her doorbell in the early hours of the morning for a laugh. Strangers came up to her in the street to offer remarks or ask questions, sometimes nice ones and sometimes less pleasant ones. Then there were those who said nothing but simply gazed at her. No wonder she found this experience unnerving. 'Sometimes they just stare and you're thinking, Have I got a bogey coming out of my nose?'

There would be more fame – with all its upsides and downsides – for her very soon, as she turned away from television work for a while and began work on new music.

In the middle of the decade, Dannii parted company with Mushroom Records. She was soon snapped up by a new label – Eternal. 'I'm about to sign a new deal with a new company,' she announced in 1997. 'I've been working on a new album for the past six months and it should be released later this year. It doesn't mark a change in direction – it's still pop – but hopefully it will be a development because I'm more involved in songwriting now. It's been a while since I've released anything, but I've just signed to the Eternal label and I'll have a new single out at the end of September,' she added.

As it turned out, the single was actually released in August, and it was a big hit for her. 'All I Wanna Do' reached the top five and sold nearly 200,000 copies. It was an upbeat and highly danceable tune that played into her increasingly raunchy and adult image. As a label boss said, 'The whole point is that we want people to think, Fuck me, is that Dannii Minogue?'

She sang with passion that all she wanted to do was touch her lover and admitted that she may not be the innocent girl that some had wanted her to be. Here her art tied in nicely with her personal life: she could easily have been singing the latter lines to those who were disappointed or shocked by her *Playboy* shoot. Even the *Guardian*'s Luke Harding was impressed, writing, 'OK, so the lyrics aren't exactly Bob Dylan, but was that my foot tapping softly to Dannii's mellow Eurobeat? Er, yes.'

The single was a prelude to her third album, *Girl*, which was released in September 1997 and continued this more grown-up image for Dannii.

Billboard magazine was impressed. 'Minogue reveals impressive growth as a singer and tunesmith, diving into the set's meticulous blend of pop hooks and trendy grooves with notable finesse and confidence,' wrote Larry Flick. He praised the lead single, 'All I Wanna Do', and said it was 'indicative of an album that's free of cloying pretensions and unapologetic in its pure-pop approach to dance music'.

The fact that Kylie guest-vocalled on one of the tracks was a plus point both musically and promotionally. Allmusic produced one of its with-hindsight reviews and concluded, 'All in all, *Girl* is an exciting and forward-thinking return from a singer who most critics had long since written off. Like Janet Jackson before her, Dannii had stepped out of her famous elder sibling's shadow and emerged as an artist worth watching.'

She launched the album with a posh bash at London's Kemia Bar.

It was 'All I Wanna Do' that garnered the most admiration – not least in the shape of several awards. She received a gold award for sales of the single in Australia, and in February 1998 she landed the Best

Video for 'All I Wanna Do' at the BRMB Music Awards. She triumphantly performed the single at Sydney Mardi Gras. By the time the third single, 'Disremembrance', was released in March 1998, Dannii had earned increased credibility, not least in club land.

She toured Britain to promote her third album, *Girl*, kicking off the tour in the less than glamorous surroundings of Margate. Still, she was excited and said ahead of the first night, 'I can't wait to get on the stage with my band. I love to see the crowd let loose! With energy in the music, we'll push it to get the audience dancing – then get real personal with acoustic versions of some favourites.'

The tour saw some barnstorming performances from Dannii and her band – she concluded the 23 dates in Basingstoke. Still, she was busy and enjoying her accomplishments. Once more, Dannii responded to success in one area by relentlessly pursuing it in another too. So, in the wake of all this in 1998, she returned to the stage to play the part of Rizzo in *Grease: The Arena Spectacular*. It was produced by John Frost. Dannii was said to have been offered the female lead, Sandy, but turned it down because she found the character 'a drip' and preferred to take the more bad-girl role offered by the part of Rizzo. 'For me it was the stand-out role. It is the only role I wanted,' she said during rehearsals.

Certainly, an interview she gave to Sky television around this time suggested that the raunchy Rizzo was closer to Dannii. She said that she had watched the Tommy Lee/Pamela Anderson sex tape ten times and that when male fans at her concerts threw underpants at her she took them home with her. Also cast in this *Grease* production was her former *Home and Away* co-star Craig McLachlan as Danny, while the Sandy part was taken in the end by Jane Scali, who was, like Dannii, a graduate of *Young Talent Time*. When the tickets went on sale they sold out fast – liked greased lightning, in fact. Dannii was thrilled to be taking part, having informally rehearsed for the role even as a child, alongside her sister in the family home in Melbourne. During the rehearsals proper for the arena production, she was in fine form, and described as 'sneering, scowling and obviously enjoying herself'.

The show was a hit and, although she was playing a supporting part, Dannii was the most discussed of the cast. It had been a tiring and – quite literally – bruising experience for Dannii. 'There was a lot of dancing and it was very demanding physically,' she remembered. 'My legs ended up covered in bruises. We were doing two shows a day and I'd keep hitting the same bruises again and again. When I went to get my legs waxed, the woman thought I must have a boyfriend who was beating me up.'

She performed in the show for the final time in November 1998 in New Zealand. There she won a nomination for an MO award (the longest-running entertainment gongs in Australia) for her performance as Rizzo. So it was an emotional but ultimately triumphant final performance for Dannii.

In the years following her divorce from McMahon, Dannii was a slightly wounded person who at first trod carefully in her relationships with the opposite sex. In the wake of her divorce, she had first dated a city trader called Mark Ellis, and then, after that relationship broke up, she fell into the arms of photographer Steve Shaw, and for a while their romance looked set for long-lasting happiness. She had spoken warmly of their relationship during an interview. 'I didn't want to get into a relationship when I met Steve last September,' she said. 'It was the last thing on my mind. I am still dealing with the shit from my marriage. My marriage will stay with me for ever. It's not something I can ever forget or pretend never happened. I'll never be that innocent again. It's a big thing for me to be with somebody else. You are just going to get hurt again, because if at any point that person doesn't satisfy you – if he is not around when you want him to be there – then you are back in the same position again. That's why I didn't want to meet anyone. I'd been shattered and needed to put the pieces back together. I still wasn't ready when I met Steve, but I do believe you can't let life pass by.'

However, it was by necessity very much a long-distance love with her career meaning she was mostly based in London and Shaw's photography commitments dictating that he was mostly based in New York. Then when his work caused him to decamp even further away

– to Los Angeles, in fact – it was the final straw for the couple and they went their separate ways. Dannii's quest for a new man remained unfulfilled as another relationship ended. However, she was about to meet a new man with whom she would develop a far more serious bond and with whom she would come close to walking down aisle again.

In 1999, she fell for Formula One ace Jacques Villeneuve after meeting him at a party in Spain. Born in Quebec in 1971, Villeneuve was always destined for Formula One racing as his father and uncle (after whom he is named) were both accomplished racers themselves. He had already won three major titles when he met Dannii, including the 1997 Formula One world championship. He has since become famous in other areas, including music and marketing, though much of his involvement in those fields was ahead of him when he first met Dannii at that Spanish bash. However, he did have an unsuccessful engagement under his belt at the time, having previously planned to wed actress Sandrine Gros d'Aillon. That relationship was a thing of the past by the time he met Dannii in 1999, as was her relationship with photographer Stephen Shaw. The first public hint at their romance came in May when the renowned Formula One commentator Martin Brundle, describing Villeneuve as 'a very happy chap', described Dannii as his 'new friend'. There followed a series of newspaper reports of the relationship, complete with groaning motoring puns including 'Minogue flags down

Villeneuve' and 'Minogue gets her clutches on the Formula One hero' and even one describing her as 'in pole position' with him. The potential for motoring wordplay in newspaper reports of the relationship would be very much wrung dry in the coming months and years. Less flattering was the description of Dannii in a report about the couple's 'canoodling', which described Dannii as a 'buck-toothed chanteuse'. But at least there was some positivity when she was credited by some racing commentators as being responsible for another upsurge in his on-track form.

However, when he performed anything less than perfectly, the media were quick to attribute that to Dannii as well; one newspaper even illustrated a story about some disappointing performances from him with a large photograph of Dannii. The female partners of famous men are often blamed in this way, from 'rock wives' such as Yoko Ono to the 'WAGs' (wives and girlfriends) who followed the England football team to the 2006 World Cup. It's a cheap misogynistic ploy and you can safely guess that Dannii saw it as such.

Although not all the coverage was so critical of her, the relationship was to become the source of growing interest from the media. One news story claimed that Dannii had clashed with Villeneuve's mother, who had reportedly shrunk one of Minogue's cardigans after putting it through a hot wash cycle. Dannii was no stranger to press scrutiny, and neither was Villeneuve, who had a very straightforward and philosophical view of how to cope with it. 'If you don't want to be seen with anyone, don't walk down the street with them,' he said.

She said that she was well prepared for the attention they attracted. 'Of course, it's hurtful,' she said. 'But I've experienced it all before.' Their shared experience with fame and their shared sharp career focus were a positive factor in their love, she explained, taking a characteristically positive view of a tricky state of affairs. 'It's easier because we accept … when he goes, "Gotta go, gotta race," or when I say, "Gotta do a show," we totally understand,' she said. 'But, then again, it's really hard to make an effort to be together.'

Dannii's ex Shaw was said to be devastated to learn of her new relationship, though other stories linked him with *Ally McBeal* star Lucy Liu.

In all, they were together for more than a year and it was a fast-growing romance. Soon after their relationship began, Dannii moved into his plush, £2 million penthouse apartment in Monaco, taking her musical recording equipment with her. It was less than three months after they first met and already she was telling her closest friends that she had met 'Mr Right'. Again, the press came up with motoring puns to mark the occasion, including 'Dannii finds the love formula' and 'Dannii in the fast lane with Villeneuve'. All the same, she denied in the early days of the relationship that they would consider marriage. 'I'm too scared,' she said. 'I'm still getting over the first.'

But then, within a month of her moving in with her man, they were engaged, and she was sporting a huge diamond ring on her finger. It is thought that he rather romantically popped the question on her birthday. Perhaps the strongest sign of her happiness, though, came with the fact that for the first time in her life she was happy to ease up on her career for a while and concentrate on her personal happiness rather than her previously relentless quest for career success. For an ambitious woman like Dannii, this was a big step to take and indicative of the joy she felt with Jacques.

Were they moving too fast, though? Friends and commentators wondered whether, after rushing so fast into her relationship with McMahon only to watch that relationship ultimately flounder, Minogue might have benefited from taking it more slowly this time round.

Not that it was only Dannii who was responsible for the pace at which they were taking things: Jacques was proving keen as well. Although he was generally sensitive about questions from journalists about his private life, when asked to describe his perfect woman, he replied, 'Just look at Dannii.'

During this time, Dannii took on a perhaps surprising theatrical role: as Lady Macbeth in an Edinburgh Fringe production. Because she was a former soap and pop star, her casting in a Shakespearean play was naturally mocked in some quarters of the often snobby theatrical world, including in an article in the *Observer*, which began, 'It's true that Dannii Minogue's profession changes as frequently as her hairdo, but few could have seen this one coming.'

Seemingly as thick-skinned as ever, she let their sneers bounce off her. 'I don't really care,' she said when asked about them. 'If people want to be so limited in their ideas, I'm not going to try to change them. I can't please everyone and I've never tried to. I just want to do things that make me happy and I get a kick out of. I don't want to sit at home thinking, Oh, people might not like it, so I better not do it. I'd never have left Australia if I'd thought like that.'

Once more, we hear words that suggest Dannii sees the country of her birth as very much the small town of the globe. In shaping this view she perhaps is still smarting from the way that the country's infamous 'tall-poppy syndrome' saw its people turn on her big sister for the crime of making it big internationally. 'I only literally get to go over there once every year and I do get homesick,' she admitted though. 'My parents live over there and I have to get back once in a while to remember where I came from.'

She was following in the footsteps of her sister again. Kylie had performed in *The Caribbean Tempest* in Barbados, which was directed by Toby Gough. It was Gough who would direct Dannii in *Macbeth*, too. She was a big fan of his way of working. 'The director, Toby Gough, is outrageous,' said Dannii. 'He wants to do something totally off the wall. Something new and exciting. It's going to be totally wild – and really good for people who maybe wouldn't normally go to see Shakespeare. With this production it's really brought to you and you're involved.'

Could it be, therefore, that far from being a surprising casting for the play that Dannii – someone without a long history of taking roles in Shakespeare plays – was actually just the ticket for a place in such an imaginative, unconventional take on the story of Lady Macbeth? She thought so. 'I've had a lot of ideas about the character and found a cast that will be willing to go all the way and do the production how I want it done. The text is pretty wide open. The sexuality, for example, is all down there on the paper. But already at rehearsals other cast members have been ... completely shocked by what we're doing.'

She was coy and tantalising during publicity interviews, keen to try to hook in as many potential audience members as possible. 'I can't tell you what we're doing,' she told an interviewer. 'You'll have to come and see it. But I'm always surprised at how easy it is to shock people in this day and age. People come with this perception that it's [adopts a "luvvie" tone] *Shakespeare*. So you stand up and you speak beautifully. But when it was written there were people beheading other people and mass orgies. We're so PC in the nineties. That's why we're setting the production in the seventies so that people can relate to it, which should make it quite shocking. When I read through the play, the sexuality jumped out at me,' she added approvingly.

'It is a very violent play – Macbeth is beheaded, there is a severed head – but people are not shocked by violence any more. The sex is as important to the play as the violence, and, because people are still shocked by sex nowadays, I felt it could be used to convey the sense of drama Shakespeare intended. My character just happens to be the one who instigates a lot of the sex. She will do anything to make Macbeth king, and she manipulates him through this sexual power that she has. How else could she have influenced him to do something he does not want to do? She is so manipulative it is just frightening.'

In case the public were in any doubt at all, she rammed home the point when she concluded, 'This is a different take on Shakespeare. If you want to see a straight performance, then you should watch the Royal Shakespeare Company. We are hoping to get a lot of people coming who would not normally go to see a Shakespeare play because I'm in it and it is a bit unusual.'

So she wanted an unusual audience to watch an unusual take on an old story. There was certainly no shortage of courage at work here. What would the verdict be? The reviews were unkind in some quarters, with one damning critique headlined 'Cringe at the Fringe' and another titled 'Is this a disaster I see before me?' Soon into the play's run, there were claims in the media that she was ready to quit the production after poor ticket sales were reported. 'One of my closest friends is her director and he's having a real nightmare with her at the moment,' said a producer of another Edinburgh venture. 'Apparently she is really unhappy and thinks that she's not very good and wants to quit the show.'

However, *Macbeth* producer John Lee strongly denied this. 'What a load of old rubbish. She is absolutely delighted.'

Kylie and Jacques were seen in the audience at one performance and Dannii seemed in positive form on stage. She was enjoying her stay in Scotland, too, though she had no plans to relocate there permanently. 'It's so much healthier than London. We've all been tired out because we are getting so much oxygen here. But I have to stay in London because it's central and it's where the main recording studios and TV studios are.'

The verdicts from the critics were a mixed bag, as is so often the case. The BBC reviewer Matt Grant wrote, 'For much of the performance, she swaggers and staggers around the grass stage acting like a low-rent Jim Morrison. In her early key speeches when she persuades her husband to kill King Duncan she lacks true conviction as she ploughs through the lines without capturing their full force.'

However, the *Guardian*'s Fiachra Gibbons was more impressed. 'Minogue's disco-queen-from-hell delivery works well and the songs, particularly Mike Dimitri's droll rock and country-and-western pastiches, are very clever,' wrote Gibbons.

Now that Dannii and Jacques were engaged, the next question was when they would actually marry. Would that too be a rushed affair? It was said that they were to have a millennium wedding at Sydney Harbour, tying the knot on a luxury vessel as the new millennium was ushered in. This was not to be. Instead, they simply partied like everyone else long into the night, with sister Kylie, brother Brendan, Villeneuve's best mate Craig Pollock, Finnish F1 driver Mika Salo and his wife among their fellow revellers. It was planned that the couple would wed at some point in 2000. 'Jacques and Dannii will get married this year. But right now, he is busy with racing – he has to do a winter test race,' his spokesperson told the press.

It was thought that there were also delays due to the busy schedule of Kylie, whom Dannii was naturally keen to have present at a wedding, not just as a guest but bridesmaid.

However, by the end of January, the press were already speculating that the relationship was doomed. The *Sun* claimed there had been 'a string of bust-ups' and a friend was quoted as saying, 'They decided to cool things down for a while. They are still engaged but just want to take things a more slowly.'

It was soon rumoured that they would tie the knot during the opening period of the racing season, but Villeneuve strongly denied this. 'I keep my professional life and my private life separate,' he said. 'What kind of honeymoon would I have if I married just before the first race of the season where there would be tons of journalists?'

He was reportedly threatening to quit his British American Racing team, too. Things did not seem happy in his life; could domestic squabbles be part of it? The remainder of the year was to feature conflicting reports about the state of their relationship. The *Sun* reported that Dannii had told a men's magazine journalist that all was well and that 'Jacques gets her motoring by speaking Italian and kissing her neck'. Then they were spotted romping in a club in Ibiza.

Around this time, there was a humorous episode on a night out. Politician Donald Dewar approached Dannii and introduced himself. After a while, he turned to Villeneuve and asked what he did for a living. 'I'm a driver,' answered Villeneuve. Dewar misunderstood and turned to Dannii saying, 'Wonderful, I have a driver too!' A mildly offended Jacques put the politician right.

Ultimately, Dannii and Villeneuve were to go their separate ways. The split reportedly came about in January 2001, though it is possible it was actually earlier because in March 2001 she revealed to an interviewer that her last snog had been with someone who would appear to not be Villeneuve on New Year's Eve of 2000. 'It wasn't somebody I knew well,' she said. 'I was very excited about that! I mean, you've got to have a snog on New Year's Eve. I wasn't going to be the wallflower sitting at the side without a kiss. It was a very good snog.'

Whenever the break exactly happened, it was said to be confirmed between them after a series of tearful phone calls between Dannii and Jacques. 'Their relationship has been cooling for a while and I think they both realised that marriage was maybe not for the best,' a friend of the couple told the *Sun*. 'There have been rows as well. Their romance has been very full on since they started dating nearly two years ago. I think the honeymoon period is very much over and they have decided to call it a day. They will both remain great friends, though.'

They had grown apart, it was said. Certainly his reported preference of a night in playing fantasy games like Dungeons & Dragons ahead of a night out was said to be a contributory factor according to some sources. Dannii would later brush aside the mere suggestion of this, however. 'Do you really think we would be so shallow?'

At this point she was prepared only to confirm the split, rather than discuss in any depth the reasons for it. 'Look, we were engaged, as everyone knows, and now we're not,' she said. 'But it's amicable.'

A spokesperson for Jacques was equally vague about the reasons, confirming the split and adding only, 'They will not be releasing a statement and have no other comment to make.' Once more a relationship had failed and her touching dreams of a happy marriage had been shattered.

In time, both Dannii and Jacques would speak at more length about what went wrong. This time, though, Dannii would not be responding to the split with a *Playboy* photoshoot. Instead, she and her ex-boyfriend would be doing a fair bit of talking via the pages of the newspapers around the world, all of whom were only too happy to snap up as many of the details as they could.

First off, Villeneuve blamed his commitment to his career as the reason for his parting with Dannii. 'Nothing happened,' Villeneuve said when asked if a specific incident had prompted the split. 'There's nothing that pops out, saying, "Oh, that's the reason," or we just didn't get along or we got angry at each other, because we never did. We always got along. There was always a huge amount of respect. Racing life takes so much out of you that it's then difficult to have the energy when you get away from the racetrack to concentrate on another side of your life that includes other people. The fact that I need my independence makes relationships difficult. And the other thing is I get so focused on my racing. When you get focused on something, you use up your [emotional] energy and that can be difficult for relationships.'

Naturally, the story had been a huge deal for the media, including more puns (about their relationship hitting a roadblock or being the wrong formula for love) and a front-page headline that read, 'They should be so lucky in love, but the Minogue girls can't keep a man'. This was becoming a regular theme in newspaper covers of the sisters.

Breaking her silence on the matter, Dannii was

gloriously dismissive of this when later asked about it. 'Yeah, I heard about that,' she said wearily. 'The stupid thing is that Kylie and I have probably had no more relationships than the average modern girl. People just sort of love it if you can be seen to fail at something, when you have some degree of success at everything else. It's like, "Ha ha! She's awful at relationships!" It makes them feel better about their nine-to-five jobs and their own unhappy lives. But the thing is, modern life is not really conducive to long-lasting relationships. We're singletons now, with our own flats, our own careers and our own circle of close friends.'

It was a robust rebuttal of the speculative features, but they naturally continued to be published. The *Sunday Express* went to town on the story, offering up a 'couple counselling' feature, which speculated – often in a tongue-in-cheek style – on why Dannii and her sister had a string of failed relationships behind them. 'Have the sisters been hampered by bearing names that sound like something you might call a small dog? Maybe, when it comes to it, their loved ones can't imagine uttering their Christian names when they plight their troth.'

Dannii was much more sensible and moving in her assessment of the problem, opening her heart about the influence her parents had on her and her sister. 'Neither of us girls seems able to settle into long-term relationships or keep our men,' she admitted. 'Our parents taught Kylie and me that marriage is a fantastic institution. We look at their relationship as the standard to be achieved and don't see why we should settle for less. We aspire to that and dream of everlasting love … but we seem incapable of making it happen.'

While they had that in common, she said they had differing tastes in guys. 'When it comes to men, Kylie and I are just opposites in every way,' said Dannii. 'She likes scruffy-looking and natural men, the ones who are always on the move, the dreamers. I like clean-cut men who know where they are going. I like them to be in control of their lives. I also like the idea of committing for life, but Kylie is more spontaneous with her choice of boyfriends. She is more here, there and everywhere and can get bored with a man in a second. I like to get really stuck into a relationship. But many men have shied away from my controlling nature. I have decided men and women are just too different.'

These were raw and emotional subjects to chew over and Dannii was on the brink of tears as she turned again specifically to her broken relationship with the Formula One ace. 'It has been tough but luckily I was working on Valentine's Day,' she admitted. 'I couldn't have faced going out and seeing lots of people kissing. Splitting up with anyone is painful. I really wanted what my parents have got but now I fear that won't be.'

She conceded that her forceful nature was perhaps to blame for her failed relationship. 'I'm not perfect, I have always lived by my own rules and tried to learn from my mistakes,' she said. 'Our parents taught Kylie and me that. But, like a lot of Australian women, I don't take any nonsense from men. We are as tough as nails and independent. I am opinionated and it's never hard for me to tell a man he's wrong. I like to run the show and that scares men sometimes.'

It seemed that she was trying to identify the positives to take away from the ruins of her time with Villeneuve. Chief among these were a whole new perspective on her career. Having worked for so many years on one project after another, often feeling under pressure to take new turns or directions, she was delighted at last to have been able to take a step back and see the wood for the trees. With that sense of calm, she was able to choose her next move more wisely. 'I'd worked from the age of seven and I just didn't know what I wanted any more. I didn't know if I was doing the next job because my management wanted me to do it, because the lawyers wanted me to do it, because everyone else was making money from it or because it was something I wanted to do. I decided I needed time to get away and get some perspective, and Jacques was brilliant; he looked after me.'

Indeed, her next move – into musical theatre – was one that was directly prompted by her ex-partner's influence. In February 2001, she became the third Esméralda in the West End musical *Notre Dame de Paris*. 'He introduced me to *Notre Dame* and played me the music,' she said. 'It's like a line running through the relationship. He played the songs to me and I got into it. When I rang him to say I'd got the part, I was so excited.'

It was a strange career path for her to take in some ways, given that just a few years previously she had spoken of her disdain for the genre. 'They're so old and naff and disgusting,' she said of musicals. On taking the part she insisted that she had not changed her mind. 'No, I still don't like them,' she said. 'I don't like plays where there's dialogue and then on come dancing girls and everyone breaks into song and you think, Why? There's bits and pieces of shows that I like, but it's just not something I'd go and see of an evening.' She added that she would not normally go and watch musicals herself but might consider buying tickets to them for her grandmother. This play, she argued, had a more cross-generational appeal. 'This is what I like about this show,' she said. 'We're getting a young audience, people from kids to teenagers to my age group who'd never think of going to the theatre, who'd rather go to the movies or to the pub or go clubbing. I'd like to get some of those people to come along.' Again she was involved in an onstage production that took a daring angle on a well-known favourite.

A favourite that echoed with her, too, because in so many ways Dannii found parallels between herself and the part she was to play. She simply looked back to her teenage years to step into the mindset of her 16-year-old character. 'It's really fun revisiting how you reacted when you were 16 because physically and mentally all your reactions are different,' she said. 'I'm having to remember back many years to know what that was like again.' Dannii continued, 'Esméralda loves life, and she's constantly amazed by it, as I am. I wake up every day and I'm amazed by it. But, like a sleeping snake, step on it and life will bite you.

'She stands up for her beliefs, even though that can get her into trouble. I identify with that. And she falls for the wrong guy and all that.'

Having fallen for the wrong guy herself recently, Dannii was grateful for the distraction of work as she licked her wounds, and was also just pleased to be back at work, full stop. Her break during her time with Jacques had been uncharacteristic for such a work-driven woman. 'It's nice to be busy again, not just because of the relationship but because I've taken so much time off work,' she said.

Not that she and Villeneuve were strangers in the wake of their split. Indeed, she revealed, the Formula One hero was to be in the audience one evening. 'He's coming to see the show. We're friends, and everything's cool, but, you know, things take time.' She added that the interest in the Formula One sport that her ex-boyfriend had sparked in her would remain strong despite their split. 'I learned about it because I didn't know anything before I met Jacques. Now I've got friends in it that I met through him. Before, I thought it was a load of noisy cars and just didn't get what all the fuss was about, but I have become a fan,' she added.

Villeneuve did indeed show up to watch her, arriving on press night and therefore sitting among the mass of theatre critics who sat watching the production with their pens sharpened. It proved a less than relaxing experience for him. 'I felt so nervous for her, it was more nervous than being on the first row of the grid,' he said. 'I thought the play was very good – I've come over to London just to see it.'

He must have thought the play was very good, as he ended up seeing the production up to eight times, on one occasion sitting next to a tearfully proud Kylie in the audience. For her, watching Dannii perform on the theatrical stage was also a powerful experience. 'I had tears of pride,' Kylie said. 'I really felt very much like a big sister, which was really nice.' She noted – with admiration – how cool her sister had been prior to taking to the stage. 'Typical of my sister beforehand: no nerves,' she said. 'She's just always had that.'

So from those closest to her Dannii was receiving high praise for her performance. However, from the rather more harsh and scrutinising critics she received mixed write-ups.

A regular accusation flung at her at this point was that she seemed to be desperate for fame and would do whatever it took to stay in the public eye, as opposed to having a craft she loved. The *Mail on Sunday* was not without moments of admiration for her, but it concluded its review, 'The tiny Dannii pouts and shimmies. Though she just about carries it off, the self-consciousness of her performance must have made the capacity audience wonder how she has managed to enslave so many men.

She is the wooden heart of a bizarre production which is at times extraordinarily funny and enjoyable – for all the wrong reasons.'

The *Independent* also offered a mixed review of praise and damnation. 'Her singing is fine, she emotes with the conviction of a silent-movie vamp, and she puts on a convincing act of little-girl vulnerability when her boyfriend Phoebus is being stabbed by the horrible priest,' wrote John Walsh. 'But she moves around the vast granite stones of the cathedral and the stews of the Val d'Amour like a tiny, barefoot visiting duchess, gracing the company with her presence. You could more readily imagine her as a cosmetics buyer for Selfridges than a passionate gypsy.'

Dannii had said of her character that 'she's unaware of other people's reactions to her', but it was impossible for her to avoid these reviews as they were passed around and discussed backstage. At least she could smile when the *Sun* wrote that she 'gives fans a thigh-ful in new musical *Notre Dame de Paris* – and proves she's got anything *but* frog's legs'.

In truth, there was a fair amount of negative criticism of her part from the press. She was characteristically tough about the reception she got from the critics, shrugging it off. 'I don't think reviews are ever a great guide to what the show is,' she said. 'Unfortunately, reviews are written by people who have seen everything and walk into a show and say, "Impress me now", and that's not how you see a show.'

Her co-star, Alexis James, came out in her defence. James, who played Gringoire, said, 'She isn't a prima donna; she's done a great job. When the show first opened it featured Tina Arena, one of the best rock singers around. Coming from a pop background, everyone thought Dannii would struggle and, like everything, it has taken time because it's not an easy part to play. But she's stunning and just right for the role of Esméralda.'

It was a moving and sincere backing from her co-star, but Dannii was being forced to face the bitter realities of life treading the boards – and not just in terms of a roasting from the critics. But she could smile when, in May 2002, she won the Maxim Award for Best Stage Performance for her role of Esméralda.

One Friday night, she got the shock of her life when – as she took her final bow at the end of the show – a man jumped onto the stage and flashed her. 'I was really shocked. This guy managed to jump on stage, then flash me,' she said. It turned out to be a theatre engineer, marking his final day in the job with a prank. 'I'm still trying to get over it,' she said the following week.

She was in for another rude awakening when she was interviewed by Jonathan Ross on BBC Radio 2. The host's mockery of her began when, after complimenting her on her appearance, she snapped back, 'You shouldn't sound so surprised.'

He countered, 'I saw a picture of you looking really fat.'

Dannii was furious and said, 'He has such a way with women.'

As the interview progressed, he kept getting the name of her play wrong, and quipped that he couldn't be bothered to remember it. He asked about her split with Villeneuve and she answered, 'I don't have a love life so that's a short conversation.'

But Ross pressed on, asking, 'You're not involved with that guy or any of those racing guys?'

Dannii replied, 'I'm not a screwdriver.'

Ross then made the atmosphere icier still when he joked that he found it funny when drivers crash. At the close of the slot, he told her, 'Dannii, I feel that we haven't bonded.' He added, though, that he felt he had not said anything wrong.

'I'd hate to hear you when you're horrible,' she said.

Ross had the last word saying, 'Well thanks, Dannii, you arrived in a foul mood and left in an even fouler one.'

Despite throwing herself into her work, a few months after the split, the strain of the break-up was evident when she snapped at an interviewer who speculatively mentioned in passing that perhaps there was an added layer of heartbreak for her as the pair might have been planning to marry one day. 'Hey, you should be a private eye,' she sneered. 'Fancy you being able to work that one out. Two people who were engaged were intending to get married. I call that really smart.' Ouch.

Despite the newspapers' sneering about her trail of

broken relationships, Dannii did not feel that she was a tainted lover. 'I don't think I'm any more awful than anyone else,' she said. 'Everything is a learning experience, and you have to come to terms with that and move on. My relationship with Jacques went wrong, but that was not his fault, nor my fault. It just didn't work out.'

What of the future? she was asked. 'I'm single,' she said calmly, 'and I don't mind if I'm alone for the rest of my life.' However, she was ready physically for new romances if and when they came along. 'I feel sexier than ever,' she said. 'I feel more comfortable about my body and sexually it gets better for me each year. I know what gives me pleasure.'

She was still less than eager to discuss the reasons for her break-up with Villeneuve and not just with journalists – even her own sister admitted she was treading carefully around the subject. 'Everyone was really surprised,' Kylie said of the break-up. 'I don't know what happened. I haven't asked her but in her own time she'll talk to me. I can only sympathise and imagine what happened. I don't think she deserves it and it makes me very protective.'

In time, Kylie's sibling was ready to explore the reasons publicly and in more depth. Ultimately, Dannii put her the split down in a large part to her own immaturity. 'Yes, I was too young. I can say that now, but at the time I felt very mature,' she said a few years later. 'I'd experienced a lifetime of working and interacting with people by that age. I loved him. I thought this is a person that I really love being with and I can see myself spending the rest of my life with. And I thought people got married when they felt like that. Now I've been married and divorced, I know that you can love a person and not have to go that far.' Once she had picked herself up and dusted herself down Dannii was able to look back at the split and feel grateful that it happened. '[It] was very intense,' she said of the relationship. 'The press were everywhere. Now I think, Thank God that I didn't go through with that marriage. But I loved him and love is just something that grabs hold of you and pulls you in its direction. I don't regret a second of it. But there was so much attention and pressure on us, which ultimately broke our relationship.'

She remained in touch with Jacques and even returned regularly to Monaco. In 2003, she said of the millionaires' playground, 'He made it a friendly, nice place that I want to come back to. I'm still very good friends with him and his family. I saw Jacques three or four weeks ago at the British Grand Prix. It's only been positive stuff. There are no hard feelings there.'

Not that the rumoured rekindling of her relationship with Villeneuve was true, despite the reports. 'Very wrong,' she said when asked about it. 'He's married and is having a baby. I'm a single girl, and I've been on a few dates, but I'm going back into lockdown situation.'

Having been a famous sibling and then having had two famous partners in succession, Dannii was having to become used to living out her private life in the public eye. Having so relentlessly chased fame for so long, she was in no position to complain about this, and nor was she about to. 'No,' she said when asked if she wished it were otherwise. 'My defence mechanism is called "the show must go on". I'm sure people understand. If I'm miserable, I don't always want to share every moment with everyone. Sometimes it's too early to know what you feel about something,' she said.

She turned 30 later in the year she split from Villeneuve and this milestone coincided with many fresh important decisions and choices from Dannii. The first thing she had done once she was happy with her new man was to take her foot off the career pedal for the first time ever. 'I left lawyers, management, agents, everyone,' Dannii recalled. 'I told them, "I'm severing my ties and I don't know if I'm ever coming back." I need a break physically, mentally, spiritually, really. I'm cracking up here. I don't know what's up, what's down, where I want to be, or who I want to be with. I need to leave. This is not about money. This is not about tempting offers. It's about health, it's about sanity and it's about taking control.'

Given her age milestone, she was in increasingly reflective mood. For a while, she had stepped away from the limelight she had for so long craved and chased. 'It was so good to reflect on everything,' she said, looking back. 'Where did I want to go? What did I want to do? What foot did I want to put forward, and how was this all going to come together? The biggest question was: What makes me happy? It has really become my time to turn around, gather everything from past experience, and use it.'

Naturally, with her step aside there had been a sense of unease, too. Would she ever be able to get back into the public eye again? Or would she just be forgotten about for ever, and have to live for the rest of her life wondering whether she had voluntarily destroyed her own career. For Dannii, turning 30 left her feeling rather old – in show-business terms at least. Given the emphasis the industry places on youth, it is perhaps not surprising she felt this way but, even so, her fears here seem premature. 'I was worried I'd had my moment,' she recalled. 'I was very aware of that. And, honestly, these days, when I do a gig with all these new acts on the bill, I feel like the old woman who turns up at the end.'

But she did not feel that way for long. Indeed, having spoken of turning 30 as if it were some sort of ancient milestone, she subsequently changed her tune and presented it as the start of something exciting – not least when it came to her prospects with the opposite sex. 'There are quite a few guys trying to hit it off with me to say the least,' she said. 'I wouldn't say there is a special man in my life – it's more like special men. The guys call me all the time and text me and try to get into my good books. I'm keeping my options open. I celebrated my 30th birthday last week and I honestly feel like life is just beginning. I'm having a ball.'

As to anything more serious in the future, again she felt the positive example set by her parents' marriage weighing down heavily on her as she chewed over her own prospects of true and lasting romantic happiness. 'Every time I start a relationship, I expect they'll hurt me and leave me, and that's what happens,' she said. 'I was divorced after two years. It was so hard to mess up once; twice would be terrible. I look up to my parents, who have been in love for ever. I know it's rare, but I want that, too. I have to let go of the fear because it kills whatever relationship I get into. Fear is everyone's biggest enemy. It's exhausting.' She also dismissed the rumours that she had serious health problems that had forced her to drop out of the *Notre Dame* production. 'I was struck down with glandular fever and that knocked me off my feet for a couple of months,' she admitted. 'But, as for tales I have had eating disorders, that was a load of rubbish. There were reports I had dropped out of the show because I was so ill – both mentally and physically. I've had to learn the hard way to get over things like that and get on with life. Sometimes my health still does suffer because of all the travelling and long hours. I try to keep healthy and eat well but I can't do things like go to the gym any more because I just don't get the time. When I'm at my worst and most exhausted I just try to get lots of sleep and get back on my feet again. Sometimes it's even hard to do that.'

She emerged from the heartbreak all the more focused on her career. For her, the ups and downs of the showbiz roller coaster were part of its charm. Dannii has an inbuilt suspicion of anything resembling a nine-to-five, secure but routine existence. 'I would be devastated if all this ended tomorrow,' she said. 'I actually love the buzz and uncertainty of showbiz. Believe it or not, the only time I felt scared and unsure about things was when I was performing in the West End and I had a weekly wage that I could rely on. I'd be on the phone to my mum saying, "This just doesn't feel right: I'm paying all my bills on time and I have security." It's living normality that freaks me out. I feel more comfortable with uncertainty, as strange as that sounds.'

For Dannii, her place in this insecure industry was of paramount importance, and so she tended to shun any activities – however fun – that might distract her from continued success. 'I don't really live up the showbiz lifestyle any more compared to what I used to in the past,' she reflected. 'A few years ago I was going out to big parties and hanging out with all the stars, but there's only so long before it starts catching up with you. I decided my career was more important than all the nonsense that surrounds it. You can get carried away with all the wrong things but I have learned to focus.'

This newfound, mature perspective continued to her self-image. Dannii has often been accused of being an intensely vain woman but she says this is not the case. 'I'm not as concerned with image and looks as people might imagine,' she insisted. 'I think it's important to look good for the fans and make an effort to not look like a total scruff, but I don't run around with ten hairdressers and stylists. The pop business is totally driven by image, but you have to have the talent too. I just thank God that I've made it this far, because at the start I wondered if it would be a flash in the pan.' She concluded this reflective monologue with a typical moment of Dannii defiance: 'People were telling me that it would probably only last a year and here I am, ten years later, still enjoying the trip.'

The split with Villeneuve and its aftermath had been tough for Dannii. Perhaps what she needed was a new man to try to help her move on. Her first foray into romantic territory was said to be with millionaire businessman Michael Edwards-Hammond, the 32-year-old ex-beau of Prince Andrew's former girlfriend Caroline Stanbury. She was spotted alongside him at social events, and during one evening she sucked on a lollipop, prompting Kojak-inspired 'Who loves ya, baby?' headlines. An onlooker told a reporter, 'It's obvious she is starting to enjoy herself again.'

It was noted in some quarters that Edwards-Hammond was not unlike Villeneuve visually and a newspaper accused her of falling for 'body double syndrome'. However, she later dismissed reports that they were anything more than pals. 'He [is] just a friend,' Dannii said. 'There is no romance, full stop.'

The next man she was linked with was a 26-year-old West End theatre administrator called Tim Reed. They had actually met when the production company he worked for became involved with the *Notre Dame* production. They were seen partying together but Dannii denied they were a romantic item. 'We are not going out together,' she said. 'I am still very much single.'

Reed echoed this, saying, 'We are good friends. We go out together very occasionally, but the truth is she simply doesn't have time for boyfriends.'

Then the *Mirror* claimed that she was dating EasyJet mogul Stelios Haji-Ioannou after meeting him during a trip to Monte Carlo. 'They are very fond of one another. Dannii has been through some rough times recently and Stelios has been very kind to her,' said an unnamed source. 'Her last relationship ended badly, so she's a bit nervous about jumping into anything else so soon. But she has a good feeling about Stelios.'

But the paper sneered at this rumoured relationship, saying, 'It's a mystery to us what she sees in the EasyJet millionaire' as a play on the well-worn 'What did you first see in the millionaire …'

Then came a rumoured romp with former Bros bassist Craig Logan, who had since become a music manager but was still described bitchily by the *Mirror* as 'the ugly, dark-haired' member of the smash-hit pop band. 'They seemed really besotted,' said an onlooker who saw them at the birthday party of Australian singer Natalie Imbruglia. Next the *Mirror* reported that they were seen smooching at a theatre while watching former Spice Girl Mel B perform in *The Vagina Monologues*, a part Dannii would soon take up herself.

The newspaper then went one step further, quoting a 'perfectly placed source' as saying Dannii and Logan were engaged. 'Dannii and Craig got engaged a few weeks ago but they've been trying to keep it quiet,' said 'the source'. 'It's her third engagement and she didn't want it to get out because people might make fun of her. But Dannii and Craig do seem very much in love. For the moment, anyway.'

Dannii said that Logan's previous experiences with fame made it easier for them to make a success of their relationship. 'I think the best thing is that he's been there, done it,' she said. 'He understands the routine and the schedule. He likes staying out of the limelight now. He's a very private person and hates any sort of attention. We've been together for a while and we're very happy. I love being with him and we both just enjoy doing the normal things together when we have time.'

They were together for 16 months before the relationship ended. 'Dannii was distraught when they decided to call it a day, but she's coping,' a friend told the *Mirror*. 'She thought he was "the one" and loved every minute of their relationship but their heavy work schedules and hectic lifestyles haven't helped. Her friends have been rallying round, and so has Kylie, who speaks to her most days. They knew they both had fast-moving lives when they got together. But as they were never really apart for more than two weeks it was a successful long-distance relationship that worked for quite a while,' the friend said. 'But with Craig's commitments [as manager] with Pink, and Dannii getting ready to promote a new album it was inevitable that they'd have to move on.'

As for Dannii, she has denied some of the reports about her private life that have emerged and on occasion she prefers to remain tantalisingly vague when discussing her romantic life. 'I date men but I wouldn't say I have a boyfriend. Life's better when you have more than one guy chasing you,' she once said. 'Men call me up and ask me out on a date and I try to keep them guessing for a while. I'm definitely the kind of girl who plays hard to get. There have been a few guys in the last year but nobody serious. I like to go out with my girlfriends or go for dinner with a nice guy – I get the best of both worlds.' However, she was not one to avoid fruity moments and has described one of her favourite hotels in Scotland – the Witchery in Edinburgh – as 'the perfect lust den'. She is a fan of Scotland, and would love to spend more time there. 'I love it,' she said. 'I want to do the castle thing – hire a castle, get your friends and do the whole murder-mystery thing.'

At the turn of the century, Dannii was named in a *Sydney Morning Herald* article summing up the 1990s, while, at the same time, Kylie seemed to be enjoying happier times. Her catchy and aptly named single 'Can't Get You Out of My Head' was a number-one hit in some 40 countries. Finally, following some brave career decisions, she had shrugged off the 'singing budgie' nickname that she had been stuck with since her 'I Should Be So Lucky' days. She was receiving widespread praise for her shapely bum, too, and put on a memorable performance at the opening of the Sydney Olympics. Then she began to date the sultry French actor Olivier Martinez. It seemed that her fortunes were on the up just as Dannii's were in decline. Indeed, some analysts have made the case that the two sisters always have opposing fortunes at any given point. However, despite her comparative happiness at this point, Kylie predicted that her sister would be the first of the two to become a mother; and so would there be another romance on the horizon? she was asked. 'Two points,' she said. 'First, Kylie just wants me to have a baby so she can be an auntie, the same reason why I want her to be a mother. And, second, I wouldn't consider having a child unless I was in the stable relationship.' Which was not where she was at this point in her life.

Footloose and fancy-free, Dannii was certainly having fun and admitted that heavy partying was a pastime that held a certain amount of appeal for her. 'Debauchery is a good thing,' she told a men's magazine. 'Alcohol and men are my biggest vices. It means mad nights out with your friends when you drink too much and dance. The worst I ever got was in Tokyo. I'd been taken out to a club to perform and ended up so drunk on sake I had a "Fear and Loathing" moment in the hotel. I was so scared of the carpet I had to crawl along the corridors on my hands and knees trying my key in every door till I found my room.' She added happily that her relative lack of fame – when compared with that enjoyed by sister Kylie – made it easier for her to truly party and let her hair down. 'She can have all that fame because I wouldn't want it for the world,' said Dannii. 'I love my sister and am so proud of everything she has achieved, but she does pay a certain price. She is always in the papers and doesn't have a private life, and I know that sometimes gets her down. The worst thing is every time she does anything it's made into a big deal by the media. I am lucky because the level of interest in me isn't so intense. I can date guys and go out and party and it isn't all over the papers, so I have more fun that way.'

But not all parts of her life were so fun, and she was about to be reminded bitterly of the cost of fame.

In 2002, Dannii sat down for an interview with the men's magazine GQ. She had given numerous interviews to magazines over the previous ten years and had usually proved to be a pro at the art of being a successful interviewee. She knew when to reveal, when to conceal. She would say enough to make sure the resulting article was colourful and interesting, but would not usually say anything that could get her in any serious trouble. Nor did she usually say anything that could hurt others, which was no mean feat given that interviewers would almost routinely tempt her to say something disparaging about her sister. She was and is an experienced and measured interviewee, but even the most careful of celebrities cannot entirely avoid their words being taken out of context and used to create a media firestorm. The *GQ* interview quoted her as making some remarks about far-right French politician Jean-Marie Le Pen and saying that he 'struck a chord with people'. The same feature also quoted her as saying, 'Asians are pouring into Queensland' and saying of Australia that 'even some of the street signs are in Asian!' It also featured her as claiming that Britain in 2002 was 'in an appalling state with the muggings and the car-jackings'.

These were comments that strayed into slightly contentious territory, it was true. However, Dannii could not have imagined that the far-right British National Party would seize on them in the way it did. The party ran the quotes on its website under the eye-catching headline 'Kylie's sister backs the BNP'. This sensational move by the BNP invited the sort of media attention it was designed to. Suddenly, Dannii was being condemned as a racist and hypocrite, with the Anti-Nazi League reminding her that she is an immigrant to the UK herself.

She had to move fast to temper the storm, and she did, telling the Press Association that she was 'mortified' to see the BNP claim she backed them. 'I'm really, really upset about it,' she said. 'Australia is the most multicultural melting pot of people. I'm completely proud of that. I grew up in Melbourne where mostly the people around where I lived were Greeks and Italians which I absolutely loved. And I said in parts of Queensland there's lots of Asians and, you know, yes, it's true some street signs are in Asian. I wasn't saying that was a bad thing. I'm mortified that I'm being connected with this website.' Asked specifically how she felt about the number of Asian immigrants in Australia she said, 'I can't comment on the number of Asians around.'

Asked about her comments about the popularity of Le Pen, she again tried to distance herself from the spin that was being put on her words. 'I'm not understanding [the popularity] as far as that I'm siding with anyone,' she said. 'But I'm saying that the fact that he has become popular, he must have struck a chord with people. People don't follow someone for no reason. I'm not siding with the people that are following him, I don't agree with what he's saying, I don't follow him at all. That's an observation, the same as the observation that there's street signs in Australia that are in Asian.' Minogue even mentioned the possibility of legal action over the matter.

The British National Party insisted it had nothing to fear from legal action. 'We only reproduced exactly what we read in *GQ* magazine, so we have nothing to worry about,' a spokesman said. 'We don't want to be discourteous to the poor girl, but why should she be worried by speaking her feelings? Anyway, we've got people in the BNP who are far better musicians. We're into serious good white music like Mozart and Bach,' the spokesman added.

As for Dannii, she was savvy enough to know that even a robust statement such as hers would reach only some of the people who had heard of the initial controversy, so she returned to the issue. In an interview with *Gay Times* magazine, she said, 'I am not a racist. That is not how I live my life. I have a Jewish manager, I perform in gay clubs, I come from a multicultural background and I am very proud of that.'

As recently as 2007, in a feature about *The X Factor*, this part of her life was again dragged up by the press. In fairness, the issue of race relations is one she was ill-advised to stray into in the way she did. There have been no suggestions since that she has any sympathy at all with any form of racial discrimination.

Given the mention of her interview with *Gay Times*, this is perhaps an appropriate point at which to reflect on her enormous popularity with a gay audience and her sterling support for gay-rights causes. She denied that her support for this cause came from anything but the sincerest of motivations. 'Gays have always been a part of my music,' said Dannii. 'I have never jumped on the pink bandwagon to increase my popularity. It just came naturally.' Speaking of the campaigns for gay people to be given civil-partnership rights, she said, 'Some kind of certificate of commitment is important. It doesn't have to be a marriage. Something official that is accepted by all government bodies would be sufficient. As long as you can have a special day together that is recognised by the government is what counts.'

She has played at numerous gay venues and events. For instance, she stood alongside drag queens Mitzi

Macintosh and Trudy Valentine at the launch of her single 'Everlasting Night', which was the 1999 Sydney Mardi Gras anthem and also spearheaded the launch of the Mardi Gras recording label. And a scene from the promotional video for 'Everlasting Night' had been filmed at a venue called Home, which is popular among drag queens. Crowds of gay fans had queued for hours for the chance to meet her at the launch. One said, 'I admire her for supporting gay rights, which is a risk for her artistically.'

In fact, she courted controversy in the video for 'Everlasting Night', when she was featured kissing another woman. 'There is a lesbian element to it – scenes with myself and a girl called Sheridan – but it's not confrontational, it's not done in a really raunchy way. It's not like a Madonna video where she's tongue-kissing some girl on a hotel bed,' said Dannii. 'It's not for shock value.' Warming to this theme, she added, 'The kisses [in the video] are not passionate. It's just a kiss to say "hi",' she said. 'If someone criticises the video they should maybe think back to every New Year's Eve when it hits 12 o'clock and you're kissing people around you. You don't know who they are and it's not sexual or anything like that … it's just all done in fun.' She has admitted during an interview with *Glamour* magazine that she has kissed a girl. 'She's a friend of mine so it was a bit stupid,' she said. 'It wasn't better or worse than kissing a man, but not really my thing.'

Even those lesbians who were featured in the video

were deliberately cast to counter stereotypes, so they did not 'all look like dykes on bikes, they're not all running around in leather. Lesbian girls can look like whatever,' she said. Again fending off suggestions that she had deliberately tried to spark headlines with the content of the video, she firmly pointed the finger elsewhere. 'Those rap videos talking about hos and bitches, I find that far more disturbing,' she said.

'That's such a stereotype of lesbians and it's just not true. It was fun to put my neck on the line for someone else. Down the track it might have an effect on my career, but I don't care. I'd rather do something I believe in.'

Two years earlier, Dannii had joined other celebrities – including Barbara Windsor, Peter Andre and Gina G – at an open-air concert on Clapham Common that marked the climax of a huge gay-rights march through London. This was not the first time she had appeared at such a bash. In 1995 she joined D:Ream and Boy George, among others, at the Victoria Park Gay Pride concert. With more than 150,000 people in the audience, this was the biggest Gay Pride event in England at that point. The next year she was at another British Gay Pride event and captured the attention with a new blonde hairstyle. When – in 1997 – she played at Gay Pride again, she joked that Kylie had better things to do than be there. It was the same story at Gay Pride events Down Under. She has appeared at so many Australian events down the years that when the *Sydney*

Morning Herald ran a feature about Gay Pride concerts they described her as 'the perennial Dannii Minogue'. Perhaps her most memorable such involvement came in March 1998, when she took part in the world's biggest gay and lesbian festival to date. With more than a million spectators in Sydney, it was a star-studded affair. Top of the bill was supposed to be a duet between Australia's two biggest gay icons, Dannii and her sister Kylie. Instead, they appeared separately, with two hours separating their sets. All the same, they were watched by a million adoring gay fans and others too, including their parents, who stood proudly in the audience. 'Wow! It's just one amazing gig,' said Dannii. 'Kylie is already a gay icon; maybe they'll make me one now after this.'

All the same, the press soon claimed that behind their change of heart over the duet had been a huge bust-up between the siblings. Days later they posed for photographs together at a party and – as a gesture of denial of the bust-up reports – waved a tabloid newspaper at the audience and said, 'Don't read this!'

Keen to maintain her newfound gay-icon stature, Dannii took a support slot for British gay singer Boy George at the Royal Albert Hall three months later. She played the game well, cheekily asking the audience, 'Are there any queens in the house?' She naturally received a hearty cheer from the spectators in response, as did incidentally George himself when he later urged them to 'shake your poontang'.

She has been appointed the Ambassador for Young

People for the Terrence Higgins Trust – the HIV charity. She helped launch its Wear Your Ribbon campaign to tie in with World AIDS Day. 'It takes politicians, it takes schoolteachers, it takes parents, it takes volunteers,' she said of the efforts to beat HIV. 'The charity can't survive or do it alone, but I want to try to help and get the message across. The charity have an incredible team of volunteers and this terrifying disease can be controlled, but it takes education, something every one of us deserves. Every single penny counts and directly helps thousands of British people with HIV live better.'

For the charity, Dannii's endorsement was a major plus. 'We're really excited that Dannii is working with us to get safer-sex messages out to young people. She's a brilliant role model for teenagers and her energy and empathy are a great asset to our work,' said Genevieve Clark of the Terrence Higgins Trust.

In 2005, she headlined the seventh Annual Gay Day at Paramount's Great America. A portion of all proceeds were donated to an AIDS foundation. She belted out a half-hour set, including a cover of the classic Blondie track 'Heart of Glass'. Her courting of a gay audience did not come without its protests. She would often receive complaints from antigay groups when she appeared at Mardi Gras and gay-pride events. 'I'll just float along like a bimbo,' she asked about this ahead of such an event. 'That's the best way to cope with childish criticism. They criticise me no matter what, so I ignore it.'

But Dannii's love of the gay community has not always been reciprocated. When she and rock singer Jimmy Barnes were put forward as performers at the 1999 Mardi Gras event, one gay newspaper featured a letter written by a community member who was less than impressed at the choices. 'What in God's name do these people mean to the gay and lesbian community?' asked the letter. The letter was seized on by the mainstream press, with one newspaper headlining the story 'Straight into controversy'.

In her musical career, it was high time for a new release from Dannii. Her next single, "Who Do You Love Now?", was released on 19 November 2001. As the media enjoyed reminding her, it was nearly eight years since she enjoyed her last hit single. Not that she was precious about her back catalogue – she confessed that some of it left her cold. 'I cringe at some of my music because I was so young,' Dannii said. 'But at the same time it is incredible that I am still around and I am very proud. Pete Tong's label called me up about the instrumental track "Who Do You Love Now?", which had been going great in the clubs and asked me if I wanted to do a vocal on it. I really loved it.'

The *Sunday Mirror* loved it too, awarding it nine marks out of ten and writing that, with it, Dannii 'upstages her big sis with a big fat one'. *Sound Generator* described it as a 'nice serene and dreamy vocal on the dance floor anthem'. The *Birmingham*

Evening Mail's reviewer was similarly impressed, asserting: 'If there's any justice, "Who Do You Love Now?" will leave Dan up there with the big-hitters.'

There was justice and, after strong early sales, the single entered the chart at number three. In America it reached number one on the United States' *Billboard* Dance Club chart. 'It's a dream come true and I could never have planned all this,' she said with a smile. 'It's strange that it's taken so long but now I've found a place where I feel comfortable and where the audience is on the same wavelength too. I guess I've finally found that special ingredient in me that means I can put my stamp on tracks and make them individual. I don't want to lose that but I don't want to rely on sticking to a formula, either, so my new tracks will be the big test for me.'

Back on stage, in 2002, she appeared in the long-running play *The Vagina Monologues*. She joined an army of female artists who have performed the play, including Honor Blackman, Sophie Dahl, Whoopi Goldberg, Jerry Hall, Maureen Lipman, Sharon Osbourne and Kate Winslet. These were hallowed names to be listed alongside. Dannii received much praise for her take on the part, including from the *Daily Star*. 'She looked last night as if she is about to overtake sister Kylie in the fame stakes,' said the review of the first night. She was truly interactive in her approach to feedback and along with the production team she sought online critiques to tailor the performance to what the audience wanted to see. 'When I was in *The Vagina*

Monologues, the producers had a site for it and people who had seen it would leave suggestions and comments on it and they would often rewrite our script based on some of those things,' she recalled.

She had another Top 10 hit with her next single, "Put the Needle On It", released in November 2002. The initial release date was 28 October and therefore set to put it head to head with the new single by none other than her sister Kylie. 'It was never our intention to go head to head with Kylie, it simply worked out that way,' said a spokesman from Dannii's record label, as the media leaped on this sibling-rivalry story. 'The video was delayed and we only finished it on Friday. October 28 then emerged as the best release date and it was then we realised that Kylie's single was out on the same day. Dannii loves Kylie and vice versa so I'm sure if there's any rivalry it will be friendly. It will be very interesting to see how things work out. We believe Dannii will have a massive hit. A lot of people will be very surprised by what they hear.'

With the memories of the mid-1990s chart battle between Britpop giants Oasis and Blur still fresh, the media were ready to whip this release day head to head to high heaven. As it happened, Kylie delayed her single, so the battle never happened. 'She will be chilling in Australia – she has been working really hard lately,' said Dannii, explaining Kylie's decision. 'So she said to me, "OK, you take the baton now, it's your turn to run with it and do your best." Of course there is

competition between us – like there is with any two
people in the music business. But it's good-natured stuff
and there are no catfights. We give each other a break
when we need it.'

The *Herald Sun* newspaper was disappointed: 'It's a
shame they chickened out – it would have been very
interesting to see who would have come out on top.'

Dannii's promotional jaunt for the single could
scarcely have been in sharper contrast to the experiences
of her sister. On one night Dannii played a small pub in
Byker, Newcastle. The Cluny pub was a million miles
from the sort of prestigious venues Kylie could fill with
the click of a finger. Strangely, Dannii felt more nervous
the smaller the crowd she was playing to. 'I'm totally
excited about it, but pretty nervous too,' said Dannii in
the build-up to the pub gig. 'I've done big arenas and
small theatres promoting things in the past. And I've
also played small theatres with my stage work, such as
the play *The Vagina Monologues*, to just 400 people a
night. Now that was pretty scary. The more intimate
gigs are a little more nerve-racking. And this is small.
About 250 people, I think.'

Ahead of the gig she had dinner at the Treacle Moon
on Newcastle's Quayside and was delighted to learn that
an Australian chef had prepared it. She brought the
house down with her performance at the Cluny. Many
of the audience were clearly there only to see her and left
as soon as her slot was over. Later she played another
small venue in the form of Sheffield's BRB pub, although

these small venues were not something Dannii would need to get used to for very long.

Her fourth album was called *Neon Nights*. She worked with some credible producers, some of whom she had met during trips to Ibiza. It was visits to that party island around the turn of the century that had first really turned her towards a more dance-orientated sound. 'Friends had been going to Ibiza for years, but it wasn't until I went myself that it finally all made sense,' she said. 'Then I realised that it's the place where all the DJs come together and where all the music that's going to matter over the next 12 months is tried and tested. It's an amazing place to be and I still have to go there every year because I feel like I need that contact with the DJs because they're such style makers. It's important to me to know what they're up to and peek into their record bags!'

The producers she met there included Ian Masterson, Korpi & Blackcell, Neïmo and Terry Ronald. She also roped in the celebrated New York dance producer Roger Sanchez. The cover hinted at a yearning for 'cred' as well. It was a classy, almost moody affair with Dannii sitting on a bed against a plain background in a black dress. She seems to be about to remove one of her gold high-heel shoes as she gazes moodily at the camera. A more colourful and poppy alternate cover featured one shoe already off and the other about to join it. This time the image is shot from above and she stares up at the camera. The lettering on the second cover is in pink and blue, unlike the moodier original, which featured a white font.

She had been involved much more in songwriting for this album and was pleased to have taken such a plunge. 'I took everything I'd seen and heard in London and just went away from it all and focused,' she said. 'I'd done writing before, but nothing like this. I knew I could fall flat on my face but I'm an all-or-nothing person. I had to give it a go rather than regret not trying it, so I hung around studios, learned from other people and then had a stab at it myself. Thankfully, that album got a whole different kind of attention and respect and great sales, too. It was pretty terrifying but it made me realise it was OK to be in control and have an opinion on every aspect of the creative process. Now writing and producing is the biggest part of what I do.'

As it was her first fresh studio album for six years, it was naturally eagerly anticipated and then heavily scrutinised. The release came off the back of three single releases all of which reached the Top 10. Dannii was bouncing back in style with the singles – what would the reaction be to her new album? Commercially, it was to be a success but before that could be confirmed she had to face the music from the critics. Some were impressed but many were damning. Few managed to resist the temptation to hook their reviews around comparisons between Dannii and Kylie. One can imagine her rolling eyes as she read many of them. Not that such comparisons were all unfavourable to the younger

Minogue sister – not by any means. For instance, the BBC website predicted good things for Dannii as a result of *Neon Nights*. 'It may seem odd to imagine Kylie's position to be threatened by her sister, given that Dannii hasn't released an album in six years, but *Neon Nights* could just give her a run for her money,' wrote Jack Smith, describing *Neon Nights* as 'a pleasant cocktail of pop sophistication, club culture and accessibility'.

The Age – an Australian title – said, 'The album's stand-out track is "Put the Needle On It", co-written by Dannii and described by her as "futuristic retro-pop/electro-pop". Whatever. It's actually a jaunty, syncopated, pantie-dampening ode to sex …' The newspaper concluded her latest material was: 'Pretty harmless, really.'

The *Mail on Sunday*: 'It is actually extremely good: gutsy and passionate.'

The *Coventry Evening Telegraph* said that it was impossible to judge the album by any criteria other than a comparison with her sister's material: 'It's an ultra-slick combination of current pop and club themes, the territory over which Kylie has claimed complete dominion in the last couple of years, but smacks of over-production. Songs like "Put the Needle On It" and "Who Do You Love Now?" are enjoyable enough but, like everybody else in the genre, simply can't match the vivacity and charm of the market leader.'

'*Neon Nights* is packed with the same sort of high-tech, high-energy Euro dance-pop that is Kylie's calling card,' reflected the *Gazette*, a Canadian journal.

The *Seattle Weekly*, too, could not resist the temptation to lump her in with her sister as it evaluated *Neon Nights*. 'Nothing remotely groundbreaking here, but if you've invested in Kylie couture, Dannii is a must-have accessory,' wrote the paper's critic.

Even in the Asian press Dannii was unable to avoid sibling comparisons when she read the write-ups of her new work. The *New Straits Times* of Malaysia wrote: 'Between both the Minogue sisters, they have attempted more comebacks than TV re-runs. Well, what did you expect? The younger Minogue's album is an imitation-flattering reworking of sister Kylie's better received comeback album.'

If she was frustrated by the comparisons, then at least she could see that she was being supported by her fans in at least one case. *Entertainment Weekly* had been disparaging and gave the album a 'C' rating, saying, 'Minogue needs some of her big sister's cheekiness.'

Disappointing for Dannii, but she could be pleased to learn that a fan wrote to the newspaper's letters page to stick up for her and to protest at the customary Kylie comparison. 'This is one of the best dance/electro-pop/funk CDs to come out in ages,' wrote Anthony Jason Bonn. 'I highly disagree with your C rating. Dannii is not Kylie. Just because they are sisters, one shouldn't expect their music to be the same.'

The *Daily Mail* was also typically damning. 'The steamy rhythmic romps that dominate this album have more in common with the pouting pop of fellow

Australian singer Holly Valance than the classier moves of sister Kylie,' it said. ' "Put the Needle On It" uses sassy, Prince-lite stylings, but most of these tracks are dull and formulaic.'

Meanwhile, the *Sun* described one of the album's tracks – 'Vibe On' – as perhaps the worst song ever written. That must have hurt even the thick-skinned Dannii.

The *Observer* managed at least an original approach to the Kylie comparison, but made it all the same. 'If only Dannii Minogue sang madrigals or made avant-garde hip-hop, we might not be forced to compare her work with that of her sister, Kylie,' wrote Kitty Empire. 'But it's impossible not to see Kylie's brilliant "Can't Get You Out of My Head" reflected in *Neon Nights*' titanium-edged disco. You can almost picture Dannii standing over her producers, demanding even more timely electro squelches, cleverer studio tricks and saucier lyrics than Minogue Sr. The result is a record that's enormously effective in harnessing pop from the prevailing trends in clubland (the disco revival, electroclash, Eighties pop) but frantic and obvious with it.'

On and on came more negative reviews, some of which were very hurtful. Phrases like 'tired, uninspired waste of space', 'painful and cringe-worthy', 'irritating and desperate' and 'sadly pathetic' appeared in the write-ups.

Thank goodness, then, for Ian Hyland, who gave

Neon Nights 9/10 in the *Sunday Mirror* and commented, 'Better not stay away too long, Kylie.'

One of the better reviews came in the *Scotsman*. Fiona Shepherd wrote, 'The fact that [Dannii] has made a better record than her sister has ever mustered should, but probably won't, count in her favour. Kylie simpered on about [her album] *Light Years*; Dannii's domain is *Neon Nights*. The album is a homage to the lure of the nightclub, more particularly to the bit of rough she has pulled at the club and the resultant action-packed night. And, look, there she is on the sleeve in her gladrags, party shoes coming off, hair dishevelled and body language amenable, to say the least, in a succession of photographs conceived to look like amateur porn shots.' Back to the music, though: 'On *Neon Nights*, Minogue is rampant. "Take a deep drag of me," she generously invites on the filthy, breathless, textbook electro of Creep. Nods to "big red love" and "givin' me vibrations" abound, without coquettish preamble.'

The Scottish press seemed generally fond of the release, with the *Daily Record* making *Neon Nights* its album of the week and concluding, 'There's a reason X Factor judge Dannii is still going strong. Releases such as this prove she still knows how it all works. Hits, such as "Put the Needle On It" and new tracks will keep you dancing round the living room for hours.'

Meanwhile, Amazon.com's staff critic David Trueman was impressed overall as well, saying it ticked a rare box: '*Neon Nights* is for the most part a consistently good album, another unusual thing in pop music.'

The single 'I Begin to Wonder' received lots of radio play in several territories. 'I recently did my first promotional trip to Canada,' she said. 'People are liking and responding to this album.'

Despite some critical savaging in some areas, Dannii was, overall, very happy with the response to *Neon Nights*, which included RTE's assertion that 'here it seems the younger sister may be finally giving pop queen Kylie a run for her money'.

She kept it upbeat. 'Yeah, I'm really happy,' she said. 'It's, like, the best reaction I've ever had to an album, and it's not even out yet! I guess the elation is higher because I had been nervous about writing,' she says. 'If you fail doing that, you doubly fail, but I thought it was time to walk the tightrope and give it a go.' Not that she had included any of her own work just for the sake of it. She insisted that all the tracks be selected on merit alone. 'I said to the record company, 'Just let me have a go at it, and see if the songs turn out any good.' I didn't want to put them on just because they're my songs. It's a hard market out there and if I got songs from other people that were better I would have been more than happy to use them. It's been incredibly flattering to get good reviews and also good sales on my album,' she says. 'You know, sometimes you get critically acclaimed and you don't sell anything, or you sell a lot and journalists are trashing it, but it seems to be a good vibe all around and hopefully I just, I don't know, hit the nail on the head or got the formula right, and I think that was a matter of really taking time and not rushing it.'

Speaking of *Neon Nights*, she said, 'This is the real Dannii Minogue. It's fun, and it's sexy, and it's the most of me I've ever put into an album.'

It reached number eight in the UK album charts and achieved gold status. Elsewhere – particularly Australia and Japan – it did not perform so well at all.

The above reviews are helpful in capturing the mood of the moment that the album was released in, but, for the longer-term view of Dannii's life and career, a wider view is needed. *Neon Nights* was a huge step in the direction Dannii wanted to move in but, ultimately, it did not fulfil her wildest dreams. If she had set two targets – a realistic one and a shoot-for-the-moon one – then it pretty much would have fulfilled the former but would have fallen far short of the latter. Still, she ploughed on.

And in July 2003 she performed to 100,000 fans as part of Capital's Party in the Park. There was a similar-sized crowd at the T4 Pop Beach Party, where she topped the bill. There was another triumph for Dannii when her single 'I Begin to Wonder' soared to the summit of four club charts simultaneously. This vindicated her decision to plough a more club-based path, rather than relying on the bubble-gum pop route. In the mainstream UK chart, the single nearly made the top as well, reaching number two. She was handed the

Capital Rhythm Award at the Capital FM Awards for her contribution to dance music. Then 'Don't Wanna Lose This Feeling' was a top five hit for her.

Also in 2003 she was named the Best Female Artist at the Disney Channel Awards. Within weeks of that, she was in America promoting her music again, including with an appearance on *The Howard Stern Show*. She also played open-air events around the country including in New York and Miami. She was nominated for awards in American honours lists including the WMC International Dance Music Awards and the Dancestar 2004 Awards. Her fame was spreading round the world – she even reached the cover of the Indian edition of *Elle* magazine. Then in May 2004 she flew to South Africa to take part in the Unite Against Hunger, a food-crisis relief programme, headed by food and healthcare giant Tiger Brands. She sang for Nelson Mandela and within days was sharing the bill with the rather less exciting Right Said Fred. For both performances she had the audiences eating out of her hand. She then released new material in Germany and performed and presented an award at the 2004 Viva Comet Awards in Budapest. Happy days indeed and a wonderful feeling for Dannii as her hard work and confident judgement all paid off at once. She had stayed true to her artistic and commercial instincts and was being handsomely rewarded at last.

Neon Nights had proved a success chart-wise. It was certified gold in the UK where it reached number eight.

The album was put into perspective by the Allmusic website, which reflected in its retrospective review some years later: 'Without a doubt the most confident and forward-thinking release yet for Dannii, it didn't quite make her the major star it should have, but it did give her the best run of hits of her career, and continued to show she was much more than the sum of her family name.'

The material also gave her some fresh success in America, where 'Put the Needle On It' got some valuable radio play. Three months after the release of *Neon Nights*, Dannii kicked off a radio show of the same name in which she played happy feel-good songs and also showcased up-and-coming DJs. Here she showed that, far from being a star who kicks away the ladder of success once they have ascended it, she did instead hold out a hand to others in the hope of helping them to greater heights. For Dannii is, at heart, a generous and supportive soul. She was about to demonstrate this heartily as a terrible development shook the Minogue family just as Dannii was building a head of steam in her musical career and overall level of public recognition. For a while all the career concerns of both her and her sister would mean absolutely nothing to either of them.

CHAPTER SIX

saving kylie

In May 2005, Dannii was busy with her music career and was also taking part in some charity initiatives. After two successive heartbreaks, her personal life was more tranquil than it had been for some time, and she seemed happier than she had been for a long while. Then her happiness disappeared in an instant when she took a life-changing phone call from her parents one day. They gave her the devastating news that Kylie had been diagnosed with breast cancer.

Immediately, all she could think of was returning to Australia to be at the side of her sister, brother and parents. She had a long and harrowing journey ahead of her. 'My parents phoned me and all I could think of was that I needed to be with them – now,' she remembered. It could not be that simple, however. First she had to fly back to Melbourne. She was on the first flight she could get. 'Of course it's at least a 26-hour flight away. So just dealing with the shock, packing a bag, it was the longest flight, as you can imagine.'

During a break in the flight, she was to face the harsh reality of being a famous person near the centre of the biggest celebrity story for years. 'You have to refuel at Hong Kong, so getting off at Hong Kong, going to the lounge and then somebody at the lounge says, "There's a film crew here they're trying to get an interview with you," ' she recalled. 'But they could see I was in such shock and I said, "Can you please just get me to the plane without having to speak to them because I haven't spoken to my sister yet ... I can't speak to anyone before I've spoken to her – that's insane." ' At this point in her interview with Piers Morgan she broke down, as the emotion returned. She composed herself and recalled what happened next. 'So we got on those buggies that go through the airport and this film crew was chasing me and all I wanted to do was see my gorgeous sister and hug her.'

Finally, more than a full day and night after she set off, she arrived home, where family and close friends had gathered to comfort her sister. The moment she fell into her sister's arms was an emotional one, as she explained when asked what she had said to Kylie at that moment. 'I don't even remember; it was just a blur, but it was more about just giving her a hug and supporting her,' she said. 'She was scared. At the time, I just thought, however scary this is for all of us, I think it's gotta be the hardest for the parents. It's got to be.'

This scary period had begun soon after Kylie had begun to feel strange while on tour. She began to get cold sweats, causing increasing alarm about what was causing them. Then she began vomiting frequently. At first she and those around her hoped this was merely caused by the tight corset she was wearing for part of the set. The corset was encrusted with jewels and had been painstakingly hand-sewn for the tour. At only 16 inches around the waist, it was indeed a very tight fit. In retrospect, she told friends, she had been feeling run down in the weeks leading to the tour and wondered at the time whether she was too old for the pop game. As the sweats and sickness increased, that fatigue began to take on a new and more worrying significance.

She went to see a doctor but was given the all-clear. As she later reflected ruefully, 'Because someone is in a white coat and using big medical instruments doesn't necessarily mean they're right.'

The ill health continued and she eventually went for a second opinion – and thank goodness she did, for this was a decision that might have ultimately saved her life. She later recalled how the terrible news that she had breast cancer was broken to her. 'The moment my doctor told me, I went silent,' she said. 'My mum and dad were with me, then we all went to pieces.'

She was incredibly unlucky to get breast cancer just two weeks away from her 37th birthday. It typically hits women over the age of 50; indeed only around 1 per cent of women younger than that are diagnosed with it.

So to be hit with it at her age was an extra-hard blow. She had long been a supporter of breast-cancer charities. Among her generous activities were the time in 2002 when she auctioned a black mesh bra for Britain's Breast Cancer Care, raising £2,400. Dannii too had been involved in breast-cancer fundraising. Also in 2002, she had backed the Lipstick for Life initiative, which saw specially commissioned lipsticks sold to raise funds for the Breast Cancer Campaign. She had also appeared on the *Funny Women* show alongside the likes of Mel and Sue, Maureen Lipman, Nerys Hughes and Caprice – all to raise funds for Breast Cancer Awareness Month.

This was not the first time that cancer had hit the Minogue family. Ron had suffered from prostate cancer in 2001 and the two forms of cancer have been shown to have genetic links. For Kylie, though, it was just time to try to work out what came next as she took in this enormous news. Her statement was strangely detached. 'I was so looking forward to bringing the Show Girl tour to Australian audiences and am sorry to have to disappoint my fans. Nevertheless, hopefully all will work out and I'll be back with you all soon.' She later reflected on this period and how the publicity around the story made the time harder. 'I had one day's grace when I knew and then the next day we made the announcement and then I was virtually a prisoner in the house,' she recalled. 'Not that I intended to go anywhere, but from then on I was just completely thrown into another world. It's really hard for me to express how I felt or even the chain of events. It's such a personal journey. I felt really bad for everyone around me. I'm like, "Oh my God, my poor parents." It's like a bomb's dropped. It's still sinking in. It's a very steep learning curve. I would just quietly go to my bedroom and just have 20 minutes to myself and try to deal with everything.'

Michael Gudinski said of the news, 'It has come as a shock to her, the world and to her family, but she is very fit. She is a fighter and hopes to be back doing what she loves sooner rather than later. 'It was diagnosed this morning, she's got a few tough weeks ahead of her. The one thing I know about Kylie is, she's a fighter. I'm just praying that, because the doctors found it so early, everything will be OK.'

Fighting talk also came from her partner Olivier Martinez, who told Kylie, 'This is our fight. I'm not going anywhere. I'm here for you now and nothing else matters. Just get well.'

As for Dannii, she caught the first plane back to Melbourne. 'The news is very upsetting,' she said. 'As the cancer has been diagnosed at such an early stage, we are all very optimistic that everything will be OK.' She thanked fans for their messages of support. 'I know all your kind thoughts will mean the world to her as she gets better.'

As the news spread round a shocked world, more and more reactions were forthcoming. When Elton John had been given the news, he had shouted, 'Oh, my God, the poor girl!' and picked up the phone to call her with his commiserations and support.

Australian Prime Minister John Howard, whose wife underwent surgery for cancer in 1996, publicly wished Kylie a full recovery. 'I think all Australians feel for her and wish her well and hope it has been detected in the very early stages and she will make a full recovery,' Howard said.

Her former co-star and love Jason Donovan spoke confidently of how she would react. 'I sincerely wish her well with her treatment. Kylie is a strong woman who will fight this battle on every front,' he said.

Actress Anne Charleston, who played the gravelly voiced Madge Bishop in *Neighbours*, said of the cancer news, 'It was like a stab to the heart because it happened to me at that same age.'

As for Craig McLachlan, Kylie's brother in the soap and also a co-star of Dannii's in *Home and Away* and the *Grease* arena tour, he said, 'I know she will face this with her trademark strength, persistence and resilience.'

The legendary pop producer Pete Waterman, who launched Kylie's music career in 1988, said simply, 'My heart goes out to her.'

Former Boyzone frontman Ronan Keating had lost his mum Marie to breast cancer in 1998. The Irishman said, 'When I heard, I was absolutely devastated for her – but at the same time there is so much hope.'

With Dannii and the rest of the family at her side, Kylie was put into treatment swiftly. The cancer was dealt with quickly and, just nine days ahead of her birthday, she underwent an operation to have the tumour removed. Molly Meldrum was one of the first to speak to the waiting mass of media. 'They say they caught it at an early stage and with a thing like this you can have radiotherapy,' said Meldrum.

Throughout the process, Kylie obsessively studied all the information she could about breast cancer. 'In those three days there is so much medical information to absorb, to work out what's the best treatment, who would be doing it, how it would happen – all of that.'

Meanwhile, a media circus grew around her – and grew, and grew. For instance, eight out of ten national newspapers in Britain covered their front pages with the story. The *Sun* gave it its first seven pages. In fact, media interest grew so intense that the Victoria Premier Steve Bracks was moved to remind the mass of media that there were restrictions on their conduct. 'We have very strong laws, privacy laws around medical records, about access to details, about treatment,' he told reporters today. 'These are private matters between the clinician and the patient and they are enshrined in laws as private matters. We're pleased that Kylie is able to come home, to come home to Melbourne where her family is, where her friends are and to receive the care and attention that she would need at this time.'

Dr Jenny Senior told reporters that the operation at St Francis Xavier Cabrini Hospital had been a success. 'I feel confident that we caught the cancer in time and that she is now on the road to complete recovery,' she said. 'Kylie has been the perfect patient and has charmed all my staff. I just wish I could have met her under happier circumstances. Kylie is resting after the operation and her spirits are high and she is feeling fine.' Dr Senior then thanked the Minogues and also Olivier for their support. 'They made my job very easy,' she said. 'They were so welcoming. Kylie has asked me to pass on her thanks once again to all who have expressed their love and concern for her. Your support has certainly helped her through a tough time.'

A friend of the family praised Olivier Martinez for his role during such a testing time. 'He has been fantastic and has really come through for Kylie,' said the friend. 'She hasn't had much luck with men in the past but Olivier is great for her and the family adore him. He held her hand throughout the tests and was there when she came round after the operation. We know he'll continue to be there for her throughout her recovery.'

The choice Kylie made for where to have the rest of her treatment surprised some. 'I wanted a life with my boyfriend in Paris,' she said as she moved to the French capital for her treatment.

Dannii took the Eurostar train from London to give her sister some cheer. She would gently cajole Kylie into getting out of bed and walking around; other times she would prompt singalongs of childhood favourites. It was normally on a Friday that she made the trip, with her wheely suitcase, which became nicknamed 'her dog'.

All the same, she quite understandably found herself angry and terrified during this period. 'For so long there was a voice inside my head just screaming: "Why?" ' she later admitted. 'And there really is no answer. So, whether I'll ever get to a place where I totally accept it, I don't know. There's ups and downs.' So how did she cope? 'You just got to another depth I would call it rather than a closeness. A depth. You find strength within yourself that you never thought you had because you never needed it before.' Had she, Dannii was asked, ever feared the worst – that Kylie would succumb to the illness and die? 'No,' she replied flatly. 'Never thought of it. Couldn't. You don't.' So how did she feel when the all-clear finally came and Kylie was declared to have beaten cancer? 'Well there's the all-clear and then there's the all-all-clear, as anyone who's been through cancer knows,' said Dannii. 'You get the "it's all clear now" from the operation and the "it's all clear now from the chemo". You get the six months all-clear, the one-year all-clear; the proper one is the five-year all-clear. We're not there yet. It looks incredible and, you know, she's just been so strong and in my head nothing's going to come back. It's just not going to happen.'

It had been an amazingly tough but ultimately binding experience for Dannii and her big sister. Indeed, Kylie was full of praise for Dannii's role throughout her illness, treatment and recovery. 'She was incredible when I was ill. She would put the iPod on and get me up and dancing. We've become so much closer over the past few years, we're making up for lost time.' She needed the cheering up, as she likened the treatment to nothing less than a nuclear attack. 'I can't quite articulate it. It's like a prison sentence. It's a bit like being in an atomic explosion and people asking you to describe it: "So exactly how big is the hole?" I don't think anyone who hasn't had it can understand.'

Dannii and others were able to lift her spirits with the most simple of tasks. 'It would get to five o'clock and I'd think, Oh, yes, I got through another day! If you can only have one coffee a day, it better be damn good coffee. That one little trip down the street, I'd relish that moment. "Wow, I'm out of the box!" ' When she finally recovered, Kylie exclaimed, 'Obviously someone up there likes me. Thank heavens!'

Dannii's friend Kathy Lette remembered the role played by Kylie's sister and how tough and maternal she became: 'She couldn't let any of her emotions show through because they needed her strength and that was the most difficult time of her life.' Lette added, 'She went into protective mode, like a mother hen.'

But did Dannii fear falling victim to breast cancer herself as a result of her sister's troubles? 'I don't get paranoid about cancer but I do have regular checks and I was really shocked when I read about Jade Goody,' she said in reference to the cancer-stricken *Big Brother* star. 'You should always get yourself checked. There have been so many advancements that it would be absolutely silly not to.'

In the wake of Kylie's battle, it was harder for the cynics to doubt how close the sisters were. For once, all the nagging suspicions about sibling rivalry were nowhere to be heard. Dannii was dismayed by this. 'I find it unfortunate it took the fact that Kylie went through cancer for everyone to accept I love my sister,' she said. 'I will do anything for her. We do not fight, we're not jealous, we're just sisters. That was a boring story until she got cancer. Everybody's perception of both of us changed then. Particularly me – before, people thought, She must be jealous, she must feel in Kylie's shadow. But I'm flabbergasted that it took something like cancer to change their minds. Nobody wants to believe that two sisters love each other, and it pisses me off. I've never spoken about this before because we wanted to keep that side of ourselves private. But, from Day One, people said we hated each other – and that has never, ever been the case. Nobody can describe how Kylie felt going through her illness. I've been so close to her but still don't know exactly what she must have felt. I can only ever be there to support her and that's all I've done my entire life, but nobody has wanted to believe that. A lot of other people would come out and say, "Oh, I stepped in to help Kylie out, I saved her," but I'm not like that and never will be like that.'

In June, Kylie made one of her first post-cancer appearances as a surprise guest during a performance Dannii was giving at the London gay nightclub G-A-Y.

She strolled quietly onto the stage unannounced. She was carrying a bunch of flowers to present to Dannii. Naturally, her appearance brought the house down. Kylie is of course a gay icon, as we have seen, and a wave of emotion swept the venue at first sight of her. It was a poignant moment, not least for Dannii, who was touched that Kylie chose to honour her publicly with one of her first post-cancer appearances. Kylie's next appearances came in the form of a relaxed stroll in Paris, a place in the audience at a fashion show and then a dance at a nightclub in Edinburgh. But it was the G-A-Y performance that had resonated most for Dannii, Kylie and their fans. Dannii looked back at it with fondness. 'It was amazing,' she said. 'You know, I see her all the time. But it's good for the fans to see that she's well, she's healthy and she's back on stage. I knew Kylie was going to be at the club to watch me perform because we'd spoken on the phone earlier – but I didn't know she was going to go on stage. She asked me what the set list was and when I said I was doing some of the old songs she said she wanted to come. I was thinking to myself, It's going to be a nightmare getting her in and hiding her at the club. And I warned her it would be really hot.

'I'd come off before the last song and I saw her standing at the side of the stage. I assumed she would do a runner just while I was doing the last number so she could get out without being mobbed. I had my earplugs on so I couldn't hear what people were saying around me. Then she came out on stage, which was a real surprise. For me it was about having my big sister there supporting me. She came on and was being like an older sister. She came on and said, "I have a bone to pick with you." And I said, "What? " She said, "You have to sing 'Jump to the Beat'." The pictures were so cute and I was thinking about how my grandma in Australia would love it when she saw them. It was the next day that I realised what it meant to all the fans. There was a real triumphant mood to it after the last year, seeing her standing there glowing, beaming and, of course, with a microphone in her hand.'

For Dannii, being such a publicly recognised figure, the trauma of coping with Kylie's sickness had an extra depth that the rest of the family did not have to cope with. 'It put me under such pressure because I was there for everybody's questions,' she said. 'Most times I think it really showed on my face.' Her friends confirm that Dannii was the subject of endless questions about her sister's condition back in those days. She herself said she often had to respond by shutting herself away, 'because I'm super-protective of my family anyway, and I think if Kylie asked for privacy it was because she was battling something really scary'.

Whereas Brendan could walk around without anyone knowing he was connected to one of the most famous women in the world, Dannii had no such luxury. 'Every time I got into a cab it was, "How's your sister?" You can only take so much. I wanted to switch off, because I needed to keep that energy to give to her. There was a point when I couldn't take it any more – a whole year of pressure, pressure, pressure.' The pressure had been increased unbearably when, just as Kylie was beating cancer, a friend of Dannii's was diagnosed with the same illness. For Dannii this was a horrific thing to be told. 'It was devastating news,' she explained. 'They said, if my friend hadn't come for her check-up within a month, she would not be here. She had to have drastic surgery and there were implications she had to come to terms with. It was so quick.'

As she picked up the pieces of her life following the shock of Kylie's illness, Dannii returned to her music with a new perspective. She also took up learning an instrument, motivated partly out of what for her would be a dream collaboration to make. 'If I could do a collaboration with anyone it would be with Prince,' she said. 'I've loved him for a long time – and it was kind of mad seeing him come back on the Brits. I'm learning guitar but I can't play "Purple Rain" – although I have been practising. To be honest, I'm really struggling with guitar; the triangle is the only thing I can manage at this stage.'

Her next single, 'So Under Pressure', was a nod to the pressure she had felt during Kylie's illness. It was released in the summer of 2006. The song's poignant lyrics had been inspired by watching her sister bravely battle cancer. 'I wrote this at the end of last year,' she said introducing it during a live performance. 'It was a pretty tough year for me and my family. So here it is.' She sang the song with emotion, particularly the line that went: 'I want the pain to end, I'm so under pressure.' She later explained how and why she came to pen such personal and emotional lyrics. 'I'd spent all year saying, "Everything's going to be fine, we're all strong," but then you hear in the song that some days I actually felt like I was in quicksand,' she said. 'I realised then that a songwriter should always write about what they are feeling.'

One publication was less than inspired by Dannii's heartfelt song. The Australian newspaper *Northern Territory News* poured highly sceptical scorn on the effort. 'Just when you thought Dannii Minogue couldn't try any harder to be noticed, she has written a song about how her sister's illness affected her,' it wrote. 'In the world's saddest case of famous sibling syndrome, Minogue appears to be cashing in on her sister Kylie's battle with cancer, releasing a single about how tough life has been for her since her sister announced she was battling the disease in May last year.'

The *Daily Star*'s Joe Mott gave a more favourable review on the eve of the song's release: 'Dannii Minogue is officially the queen of the club charts after notching up her seventh No. 1 in a row with her new single "So Under Pressure". The sexy 34-year-old has smashed records and become the best performing artist in the Upfront Club Chart's history.'

She launched the song with an exciting performance on the television hit show *Strictly Dance Fever*.

After the trauma of Kylie's cancer battle, there was happiness for everyone in the Minogue family in May 2006 when Dannii's brother Brendan became a father, making her an aunt for the first time. Brendan and his partner Rebecca became parents of a baby boy called Charles Sand Minogue. 'The first time I met him he screamed his head off; he was having a fit about something,' Dannii said. 'Then I got to feed him with a bottle and he farted on me. That was our first meeting, so it can only go uphill from there. Kylie was on the phone straightaway to me, asking, "What's he like? How was it?" She can't wait to see him.' She stayed in touch with her nephew wherever she was.

'My brother sends me pictures every day on email,' said the proud aunt the following month. 'He's the first grandchild for my parents so it has taken the pressure off me for a while! They are always asking when I'm going to have kids. I've got to find Mr Right first.'

As we shall see, Dannii has since found Mr Right and is now on the way to motherhood. She began to road-test some aspects of parenthood as an aunt, though she initially left some of the more testing tasks to her big sister. 'Well, I'm learning. I've got my L plates on,' she said. 'There's nappy changing and there are tears and there's playtime. Kylie's braved the nappy changing; I haven't,' she added with distaste. 'I'm like, "You're older, you go first. Show me how it's done." '

A friend of hers noted Dannii's way with Charles and said, 'I think the nephew has definitely got a few things going through her head.'

In the meantime, the wild child Dannii continued to be, well, wild. And, in 2006, there was sexual controversy aplenty when a British Sunday newspaper printed photographs of Dannii 'canoodling' with a female lap-dancer. Grainy CCTV footage showed her frolicking with a blonde stripper called Jupiter at Mayfair's Puss in Boots nightclub. Dannii was hurt by the emergence of this story, which apparently was published only at the last minute after a story about a football scandal fell through. 'She is extremely annoyed someone tried to make money from this,' said a spokesperson for Dannii. 'They were having a great laugh, but only that.'

Naturally, these words went only some of the way to calming down what was being spun as a sensational story. It was not the first time Dannii had visited the venue or the first time that her connection with it had been mentioned in print. Indeed, just months earlier she had spoken openly of her visits there and said that they had inspired her to consider installing a pole at her home. 'I'm trying to work out how my London pad can accommodate a pole, although with floor-to-ceiling windows it's probably best for the neighbours that I don't,' she said. The comment was made partly in jest, but she was less amused when the *News of the World* published their story.

Under the headline 'It's Dirty Dann-cing' on 5 February 2006, the story prompted widespread shock, not least due to the fact that the *News of the World* quite naturally went to town on it. It described in lurid detail what it described as 'gob-smacking' footage that saw Dannii 'writhe in lust' with a naked lap-dancer and clearly break the 'no-touching' rule that governs such venues. The paper even quoted an 'astonished punter' who it claimed had witnessed the goings-on first hand. 'Dannii was having the time of her life and didn't care who saw,' said the source in typical newspaper quote-speak. 'She wasn't in a private booth or the VIP area, she was on the dance floor. I can't believe how far they went. It was more like a porn film. There were hands and tongues everywhere – I thought it was going to turn into a full-on orgy.'

Another source said that during the noisy romp Dannii 'kicked her legs in the air squealing. Lots of people could hear it all.'

These were embarrassing details for Dannii to see in the public domain. She spoke out furiously in response to the stories. 'I was totally set up but it woke me up to the fact that there are some creepy, nasty people out there willing to do anything to take advantage of someone famous,' she said. Her thoughts were also going out to her family. 'Once someone publishes that,' she said, 'people you wouldn't have gone with see it – family, other friends, grandparents. I wouldn't have gone to a strip club with my grandparents, so why is it fair they see that?'

To be fair, it was an even harder time for the dancer,

who had not told her parents what she did for a living. 'She tried to keep her work life and her home life quite separate,' a friend of hers told the press. 'This has blown it.'

Her stunned mother confirmed this, saying, 'We didn't know what she did, it's come as a shock. My daughter is in bits.'

She – and Dannii – might have been embarrassed but of course the story ran and ran. Within days another dancer had come forward to the press to claim she had been raped at the venue. These were bad times for Dannii, who just wanted the entire story to be dropped. All the same, she might perhaps have drawn some comfort had she been aware that a *News of the World* reader had written to the letters page with an impressed tone. 'I never thought Dannii Minogue had much sex appeal,' wrote Dave Green of Liverpool. 'But after seeing the erotic images of her with a lap dancer called Jupiter, I've changed my mind.'

After a while, the story died down – but only for a while. In 2007, it re-emerged when the stills of the footage were published on the Internet, much to Dannii's disgust. They were circulated in viral emails that swept computers across the globe, and were also posted on a website that celebrates celebrity nudity. She hoped she had seen the back of the episode, and yet here it was again, just as she was signing up to *The X Factor* and when she was already a successful judge on *Australia's Got Talent*. Not that she was alone in receiving such unwelcome exposure. Embarrassing sex footage has been leaked of numerous celebrities, including socialite Paris Hilton and British star Jordan. As the stories about Dannii were circulating, she was firmly ensconced in the public eye and ready to take on her most mainstream position to date.

A friend was quick to defend her in the wake of the online leak. 'She signed up to X Factor because she loves music and wants to help find the next big thing,' the friend said. 'There are some really talented people this year and she doesn't want this lesbian nonsense to overshadow them. Dannii wants to make a success of her role and the last thing she needs is to be distracted by people who want to make a fool of her using the Internet.'

Accordingly, her lawyers moved to buy the copyright to the images, in the hope of gaining some sort of control of the issue.

Both instalments of the episode had been damaging. A feature in the *Sunday Express* was headlined 'Oh Dannii girl, just how far will you go?' In the feature, Camilla Tominey was damning of Dannii, arguing that, however much Dannii might attempt to laugh off the nightclub romp, 'ordinary folk will no doubt regard her behaviour as unsavoury and insensitive'. Closer to the bone was Tominey's conclusion that, 'For Kylie fans, it will confirm what they have been saying from the very beginning – that Dannii has never been, and never will be, a patch on her big sister.'

Such damning, moralistic assessments are almost inevitable from the middle-market papers such as the *Express* and *Daily Mail*. Dannii could shrug the criticism off. The story had given her an edge and in all honesty a lot of her fans may even have secretly admired her for her behaviour. In today's climate where all too many stars are becoming carefully managed and sanitised figures, the image of a celebrity letting her hair down and partying so provocatively was actually appreciated by many. Male fans appreciated the eroticism of it and female fans vicariously enjoyed her wild night.

All the same, Dannii was keen to move on from the controversy and be recognised once more for her work, rather than her social life, and so she set to work on filming the promotional video for her single; So Under Pressure;.

A surprising interest of Dannii's is in snakes. However, she had a scary moment with a python while filming the video. 'The python was on its best behaviour for most of the shoot and was curling around me beautifully,' she said of the filming. 'Everyone was thrilled. But then things started getting out of hand. It constricted itself really tightly around my waist and I couldn't breathe.'

With growing panic, Dannii was unable to speak so took to making wild gestures to the director, to try to make him realise that there was a serious problem. However, he initially assumed that, far from being a signal of a very real danger, Dannii's gesticulations were merely a sign of her getting into her stride more passionately performance-wise. Luckily for all concerned, the white python eventually released its grip.

Showing characteristic strength and attention to detail, Dannii had deliberated hard about what colour python would work best for the video. 'I thought a white one would match the outfits I wore best,' she had concluded.

Far from dreading the shoot with the seven-foot snake, she actually had looked forward to it. 'I couldn't sleep the night before the video, I was so excited. I really, really like snakes,' she said. 'It's a cream-coloured python and is apparently very rare – there are only a few in the world. I was able to have it around me and get its face really close to mine – a lot of the people on the set were like, "Oh my God" and my manager was not happy. But I loved it. It didn't have a name so we called it Liberty – and every time I see the video I think, Oh – my snake!'

It has been an ambitious brief for the video for the single 'So Under Pressure'. Indeed, the snake stunt made the title of the track come more true than she could have imagined. Dannii, though, is a brave girl and has always enjoyed some rather edgy and, yes, boyish pastimes. 'I tried to put different things in the video that made me feel under pressure and it really did!' she laughs. 'It was the hardest video I've ever done so I kept thinking, Why on earth did I come up with this concept? Actually, the one thing people tell me they couldn't do is be that close to a snake but that didn't bother me at all. It was beautiful. People don't realise but I definitely have that Australian tomboy side to me. I love snakes and sharks and jumping out of planes and stuff. Growing up, I was closer in age to my brother so it never occurred to me that it wasn't a girly thing to ride a bike, covered in mud holding frogs and collecting lizards!'

One Christmas she took the extreme side of her nature to a new level when she sought out a chance to get up close and almost personal with some sharks. 'I went to see the great white sharks – I actually went in the cage and was lowered into them,' she said. 'It took me, like, four visits before I could get up the courage, but then I went and I really enjoyed it.' That said, there are some extreme activities that she could never consider doing, as she revealed while discussing the many 'celebrity' offers that landed on her management's desk. 'Every day the phone rings with some kind of celebrity nonsense which would just freak me out,' she admitted. 'There's nothing that's come along that appeals to me, I love watching it, though – maybe if it was an extreme-sports thing I would consider it. I love *I'm a Celebrity ... Get Me Out of Here*, but I could never do it. I just couldn't do the not-eating thing, I'm scared of the dark and I've never camped before. I could jump out of the plane fine, but the other bits that people find easier I couldn't do. The thought of eating bugs – urgh.'

That said, she has long been a daredevil. When she

first moved to London, she was a little nervous about living in a big and strange metropolis. Then she got her motorcycling licence and all that changed. 'That was really cool,' she recalled with a smile. 'I used to ride around London at night – it was gorgeous. I guess I'm a bit of a tomboy really – always have been.'

She was considering a new film role at this point in a planned production called *Except East Richmond*: 'It's just a really amazing script. It's one of those roles that most female actresses want because it's not just a girl standing there and looking dumb and pretty: it's one of those roles that is integral to the whole film. It's kind of like a dark, psychological thriller – the closest film I could compare it to would be *Sixth Sense*.'

It is believed that the film has yet to receive a proper release.

In June 2006, she confirmed her stature in the music industry when she released her greatest hits compilation *The Hits and Beyond*. Dannii says it was a conversation with her sister that had prompted her to take the greatest-hits route at such a relatively young age. 'Kylie told me she wanted to hear the old songs all together, from the start through to my new dancey stuff,' said Dannii. 'So it's down to her. It was a bizarre experience putting the hits together and looking back at some of the videos. The cringe factor was pretty bad – there were fashion disasters and bad hairstyles. But I told the record company I didn't want to leave anything out. I won't lie. It's been weird putting it together, quite intense. My life on a platter. I saw Kylie last week and told her I was going crazy.'

The *Daily Record* welcomed the presence of her bigger hits but said that, as for the songs beyond that, 'only the most devoted fan will care'. As such, it did not sell as well as planned, though Dannii did her best to shrug off this disappointment. 'I've always accepted it is what it is,' she said. 'Once you've done the work, you just have to put it out there and see what happens.'

Fans of both sisters were delighted when in December 2006 Dannii performed an all-too-rare duet with Kylie. The elder Minogue was wearing a leopardskin body stocking and matching basque while Dannii oozed sex appeal too in a black basque and fishnets. The two sang 'Kids' at Melbourne's Rod Laver Arena. 'You waited a long time for this, didn't you?' Kylie asked the audience as Dannii joined her for the song. They had indeed – it was their first duet in nearly 20 years.

In the wake of this surprise duet, Dannii put out her first ever Christmas-themed song. In recording it, she took on a Welsh harpist called Amanda Whiting, whom Dannii had first spotted when she supported jazz artist Jamie Cullen in Wales two years earlier. 'She took one of my CDs and said she has been listening to it ever since, and then we got together to arrange a song,' remembered Whiting. 'Dannii was lovely. She said she would keep in touch after seeing me perform … and she has. Last week I was just walking on air.'

Their song featured on the charity album *Spirit of*

Christmas 2006, which was released in Australia in aid of the Salvation Army.

By this point, Dannii had returned Down Under for a major new project that would once again make her the toast of television viewers across the country. Her success there would then catapult her into one of the UK's biggest television shows.

CHAPTER SEVEN

battles on the box

To younger British television viewers, Dannii is known best not for her acting, nor even for her singing and modelling. To them, she is primarily known for her role as a judge on the smash-hit ITV reality series *The X Factor*. Since she first appeared as a judge for the 2007 run, she has become much loved and respected for her judging and mentoring ability. Equally, her place at the centre of numerous controversies during the production of the show has given her a new notorious reputation in the public eye. She has had to face hostile behaviour from her fellow judges on more than one occasion, and, while this rough treatment has upset her deeply at times, Dannii can at least console herself that in the court of public opinion she has been judged very favourably by most who witnessed the bitchiness and spats.

The tale of her ascendancy to the heights of television talent-show judging began in 2005, when she first met the king of this realm, Simon Cowell, at the *GQ* magazine Man of the Year Awards in London. They quickly hit it off and this is not a particular surprise. Dannii is nothing if not fiercely ambitious and focused – both qualities that almost invariably get Cowell purring. Throw in her telegenic beauty and you have a combination bound to impress him. And so it was: according to a source, Cowell quickly decided that Dannii had what it took to be a winner on his franchise of television talent shows. 'He was bowled over by her,' said the source. 'She's funny, down-to-earth and charming. He told her she's got what it takes to be a massive TV star all over the world. He wants to build a show around her.'

With Cowell's excited words of endorsement ringing in her ears, Dannii could dream of her next big career move. With Kylie not attracted to the reality-show judging path, here at last could be a career realm in which Dannii could be the pre-eminent Minogue.

Cowell first tried her out on the Australian wing of his successful *Got Talent* franchise. The first airing of the franchise was supposed to be in Britain, but in fact debuted in America. It has since appeared in Britain and up to 30 other countries including Australia. Dannii was chosen as one of three judges for the first run Down Under. She could empathise with the nervous auditionees as they turned up to perform in front of the panel. It made her look back at her own nervous auditions for various roles. The worst for her had been when she tried for the part of Esméralda in the London production of *Notre Dame*. As she took part in *Australia's Got Talent*, she looked back at that audition. 'It was at the Dominion Theatre, which is one of the biggest theatres in London,' she said. 'I had never performed on stage in London and there I was, alone on this vast, empty stage. The whole theatre was deserted apart from four people all sitting together watching me from the front row. I just walked on and started banging out a song, but I was thinking, What the hell was I thinking? What am I doing here?'

That day she got the part, but it was of course a harsh reality of shows such as *Got Talent* that most auditionees would not be so lucky. All the same, she felt that anyone who appeared on *Australia's Got Talent* would most likely take away some sort of advantage from the experience. 'People may not win, but they will get so many amazing things out of this because they have been seen by so many people,' Dannii said. 'Agents and managers have already been ringing up and trying to sign some of the performers.'

It was an attention-grabbing panel – she would be judging alongside musician-turned-television star Red Symons and cabaret star Tom Burlinson. Between them, they saw some very talented acts, some distinctly talentless acts as well as everything in between. 'Weird, wacky, wonderful – I think we have seen them all,' said

Dannii, who admits that when she watches such shows from home she mostly enjoys the more eccentric and untalented acts. 'To show you the heights we have to show the depths.'

The show aired on Sunday evenings on the Seven Network, kicking off in February 2007. Artists of all genres and ages competed for the prize of $250,000. Dannii enjoyed taking part in the show and was also pleased to have some time back in Australia. 'I've had loads of family time which has been really lovely,' she said during the production of the early stages. She enjoyed the symmetry of her new television role: 'As in, me starting off having auditioned for *Young Talent Time*, and now thinking, I'm all grown up and I'm in the judge's seat. It's a nice feeling.'

Naturally, the presence of such a national treasure as Dannii on the show attracted plenty of attention. But the critics were not always as kind to her as she was to the contestants. *MX* magazine's critic wrote, 'She couldn't have lasted this long in the public eye without a certain amount of brains but ... her stylised responses [are] cringe-worthy ... she's trying too hard to connect with the younger audience.' The article's conclusion was probably the harshest passage: 'Basing my judgement solely on its first episode, Australia has got talent, it's just not coming from Dannii Minogue ... yet.'

These were unkind words but the viewing public largely disagreed and took Dannii's performances as a judge to their hearts as they lapped up every moment of the new show. Little wonder: Dannii looked great, she judged well and showed herself to be a perfect person to tread the line between over harshness and over softness required by a judge. Furthermore, the audience could feel her empathy and wisdom as she delivered her verdicts to the hopefuls.

It is to an extent a tough life for a judge on any such reality show because few want to shout about how much they enjoy such branches of entertainment. Indeed, Dannii herself argued that *Australia's Got Talent* represented a guilty pleasure for many. 'Nobody wanted to admit they loved the show but when it rated well it made them a bit more willing to admit it,' she said ahead of the Season One final. 'I love that it's so family friendly and so much fun.'

She had been pleasantly surprised by the level of talent that Australia had during Season One – and she knew what she liked. 'I'm constantly impressed. I'm either like, that's amazing, because it's good or amazingly bad,' she said. 'People who do strange things, they're my people. I knew we'd get talent but it's the people who would never get the attention if it wasn't for this show that I love.' She loved the whole process, from the opening auditions to the tense closing stages of the show. She also enjoyed working with Cowell from the off. 'He's tough to work for and he should be: he's got a lot of people he's responsible for.'

The final would be contested between Herb Patten and Bonnie Anderson. As preparations for the

Australia's Got Talent final were under way, Dannii's work featured on another show called *Dancing with the Stars*. She performed her new single, 'He's the Greatest Dancer', on the show, but said she was not about to appear on that show as a contestant. 'It's as camp as you can get, so it's right down my alley,' she said. 'I've been asked a couple times to go on it, and it's not that I'm shy of hard work, but it would be so mentally and physically challenging. I've been doing some ballroom classes which last an hour, and that takes it out of me.' She was told that her performance on *Dancing with the Stars* was good, but she was – initially at least – unable to watch it back. 'My parents came into the studio to watch me sing but they didn't know how to work the VCR, so I couldn't see how I went,' she laughed.

Back on *Talent*, Anderson was the winning act but the real winner was, as ever, Simon Cowell, who could watch from the sidelines as his international entertainment empire notched up another success. As for Dannii, she was not surprised, she said, by the success that *Talent* had proved to be in Australia. 'It was number one in the US and France and we all wanted it to do really well in Australia,' she said. 'All my friends were asking me before the show started what makes it different from *Idol* and I said, "It's so diverse. There are musicians, acrobats and there's comedy." '

Something that had surprised her, though, was the challenge of being a judge. It had all seemed so much easier when she had sat at home watching television talent shows. The reality proved tougher. 'I didn't know how hard it would be. You can't really prepare for it, and normally I'm handed a script and can go from there,' she said. 'People were asking me whether I was going to be nice or nasty, but I just wanted to be honest with people. Once you start performing, if you're good you will go to the top, but, if not everyone likes you, then it will be hard.'

As for Dannii, she had proved herself and had gone up in Cowell's estimation. She was such a hit on *Australia's Got Talent* that he quickly lined her up for a part on his smash-hit UK talent show *The X Factor*. It was a show that Dannii had watched and enjoyed in the past and she was thrilled to be approached to take a judge's role on it. Her sister Kylie had first suggested that Dannii might be a hit on the show. 'Before I was ever chosen to be on the show,' she said, 'Kylie had been telling me, "You should do that, you'd be great at it." And I thought, Are you kidding me? But it feels right. I get great joy from seeing other people do well. My friends watch *The X Factor* and they say it just lights me up.

'Since I've done *Australia's Got Talent*, there have been requests popping up,' she said when the news of her *X Factor* role first broke. '*The X Factor* in England is massive and I was one of those people who always watched it.'

It was first reported that Dannii would replace judge Louis Walsh and sit alongside Cowell and Sharon

Osbourne on the panel. Then a rumour of a new fourth judge circulated. To complete an atmosphere of musical chairs, host Kate Thornton was replaced by Dermot O'Leary. It was a programme in flux that she was invited to join, making it an even bigger risk for her to take. Dannii has rarely been afraid of a risk, though.

She was in Australia when she was first approached about taking part in *The X Factor*. The first people she told once she confirmed her participation were her parents. It was not as exciting a moment as it might have been, because they had not actually heard of *The X Factor*; but, then, as Dannii admits, her mum and dad's entertainment knowledge had a few gaps in it. She recalled with a smile the time her parents were introduced to rock giants U2 backstage at a Kylie concert and asked them what they did for a living. Indeed, not many people Down Under had heard of *The X Factor* at that stage, she explained. 'People there don't know the show like we do, so it wasn't until I got back to London that I exploded and told all my friends and got properly excited about it,' she said.

From the first day of filming Dannii was still properly excited to be part of *The X Factor* and just could not believe her luck – so much so that she found herself wondering whether she was part of a practical joke. 'The first day of auditions was just incredible – being in with the judges was amazing. When Simon and Sharon asked for my opinion I was like, "This is brilliant." I honestly expected someone to run through the doors and for me to find out that I'd been *Punk'd*, like on MTV. I thought it was literally the most elaborate *Punk'd* ever on TV. I was in shock about just being on set.'

She was, indeed, living the dream. Ironically, one of the aspects of her new job she had most been looking forward to was meeting Sharon Osbourne. 'I'd watched *The Osbournes*, I'd watched *The X Factor* – I was a massive fan,' she remembered. 'It couldn't have been more devastating to turn up and realise she didn't want me there.'

Not that everybody was happy at her arrival at the door of reality television. Irish pop giants Boyzone had once been criticised by Dannii. In particular, she had accused Stephen Gately of singing 'through his nose'. In response to this attack, Gately had been even more stinging. 'I say it's better than speaking through your arse!' he said. 'We blackballed her. We don't like her any more. We never liked her.'

When she began work on *The X Factor*, Gately's band mate Ronan Keating said of Dannii, 'She hasn't got the X Factor any more.'

Another Boyzone member, Keith Duffy, also got involved. 'Dannii was absolutely beautiful in her day, she was gorgeous,' he said. 'She had to live in the shadow of her older sister all the time. She's trying to compete with that ... Age is an awful thing to all of us. We all get older – gravity kicks in.'

Dannii was no stranger to the rough and tumble of

public life and, in fairness, she seemed to have thrown the first stone in this incident. All the same, it served as a useful reminder that, by increasing the level of her public exposure through her place on *The X Factor*, she had opened herself to a whole new level of potential hostility. In particular, she had taken on a judging role that involved her dishing out criticism. Naturally, she would have to get used to receiving some in return and some of it would come from her fellow judges, one of whom, Louis Walsh, had managed Boyzone.

As expected, Dannii made for absolutely cracking television from the start. During the London auditions, she and Cowell clashed while discussing girl band W4. Cowell was unimpressed by the girls but Dannii countered, 'I absolutely disagree with you. The unity and your energy is amazing. It's like I want to be in your gang, I want to go wherever you go next because you look like you're going to have fun!'

It was a similar story when enthusiastic brother-and-sister double act Same Difference auditioned with an excited version of 'I'll Be There for You'. 'OK, can we lose the crazy faces, the screaming, the shouting?' asked Cowell. 'Because this is just insane at the moment. You are so funny, you two! God, I pity your parents. I bet you both wake up in great moods.'

Dannii countered, 'I don't think these guys can tone it down and I don't think you should. You guys do that so well and you're so adorable and lovable and you should keep doing that.'

Nice to see you – at Bruce Forsyth's 70th birthday celebrations.

Above: Backstage during the production of *Notre Dame de Paris*. Minogue was Esméralda.

© *Rex Features*

Right: Minogue live on stage in London.

© *Rex Features*

Above: The Minogue sisters.

Below: *Australia's got Talent* in 2010 with Westlife's Brian McFadden and Australian radio star Kyle Sandilands.

© *Rex Features*

Above: Minogue and
Simon Cowell collect
an award.

Right: A performance
from 1991.   © *Rex Features*

Above: Minogue on stage at Gay Pride in the early 1990s.   © *Rex Features*

Left: Addressing her audience.   © *Rex Features*

With Kris Smith in early 2010 and, *inset*, their house in Australia.

Above: When a princess of pop met the Prince of Wales – Charles and Minogue.
© Rex Features

Left: Minogue's arena appearance in Birmingham in 2003. *© Rex Features*

Dannii Minogue in 2010.
© *PA Photos*

Inset: Baby son Ethan was born at the Royal Women's Hospital in Melbourne in July 2010.
© *PA Photos*

Although she was nervous of her fellow judges at first, Dannii soon felt comfortable disagreeing with Cowell. 'He's great because he's up for a fight – and I'm the one to challenge him,' she said.

She was also a fan of 20-year-old contestant Sam Donaghey, who sang 'Handbags and Gladrags', telling him, 'I love your voice and its tone, I think you could sparkle. I love you, I think you're fantastic.'

She mostly enjoyed the audition round, including some of the more eccentric acts who turned up. For Dannii, this was a straightforward reflection of what she had most enjoyed in previous years as a viewer at home. 'They were amazing,' she said. 'Amazing. However, a lot of people I call my Gary Larsons – they're on the Far Side! They're on their own little planet, having fun in their own universe. But they're all really good fun. As a fan of the show, I would always tune in to see the peculiar contestants rather than see the people who were really talented. You always get everything at auditions. You can get 14,000 people coming along in one day, so you really do get all sorts.' For her, one particular act would remain long in the memory. 'We had a lady called Susan,' she recalled. 'She sang a whole song and brought me to tears! She was so funny that when I laughed my tears sprung out vertically, not downwards like when you're sad. I really tried not to laugh, but in the end all four judges were laughing. One of the crew members said to me afterwards that it's the first time that he's seen all the judges lose it at the same time. I think [Susan] thought she was at Wembley or something, though. She was in the zone. And a guy called Dwayne I loved too. He's an inventor and he's making a turbine or something to save the world. He had the longest mullet hairdo in the world – it was incredible. He has his very own sense of style.'

After the opening audition rounds, the action moved to the 'bootcamp' phase, which took place at the stately home of Heythrop Park House in Oxfordshire. For the first time in *X Factor* history, the bootcamp phase saw all the categories of acts together and this was also the first time that there were four categories: Boys (14–24); Girls (14–24); Groups and Over-25s. There were four days of auditions and deliberations before the remaining 50 finalists, plus Dannii and the other judges, moved to London's Apollo Theatre. Between them, the judges whittled the numbers down to just 24 contestants – six in each category. Once that had been completed, each judge was told by the producers which category they would be mentoring for the remainder of the series. Dannii was given the Boys group and was delighted with the news. So were the boys, including Leon Jackson – who said, 'I was thrilled to get Dannii as mentor, she is on the same wavelength' – and Rhydian Roberts. She told her six male contestants that she would be taking them to Ibiza for the judges'-houses phase of the competition. Her sidekick as she made the difficult choices to reach her final three would be producer Terry Rowland.

Once in Ibiza, all six boys sang to Dannii and Rowland and she then had to make her difficult decision overnight as to which three she would send home and which three she would keep for the forthcoming live shows. As the news was broken, there were tears and cheers in what is always a highly emotional part of the series. Dannii performed the part perfectly, drawing out the drama for the benefit of the viewers. She could call on her acting experience to really keep the contestants – and viewers – guessing as to whether a yes or no was on its way. Her final three were 22-year-old Welsh lad Andy Williams, 18-year-old Scot Leon Jackson and 24-year-old Welsh operatic star Rhydian Roberts. It was a strong final three for her to take to the live shows, but surely even Dannii could not have guessed just how strongly her category was going to perform once the show went to the public vote. Things were, on the surface, going very well for her. However, resentments and tensions were bubbling under the surface and, once the live shows kicked off, these would rise to the top and Dannii would find herself in the centre of numerous hostilities.

The pop-talent-show format was not always such a tempestuous affair as it is nowadays, but all the same tensions between judges have always been an attractive part of the genre. During the first series of *Pop Idol* in 2001, Simon Cowell and Pete Waterman often disagreed on the merits or otherwise of particular contestants. One evening on a live show they argued about a performance by finalist Darius Danesh. Cowell and Waterman are old friends but had long had the capacity to argue with each other over anything. Their onscreen bickering made for attention-grabbing television. They continued to disagree during the second series of *Pop Idol*, most notably over the eventual winner Michelle McManus. Cowell, ever the canny operator, made sure that inter-judge tension was a focal point of the show he had personally launched off the back of his *Pop Idol* success: *The X Factor*.

From Series One of the new show, the battle lines were clearly drawn. With this format, the judges did not merely offer verdicts on the performances of the contestants: they each 'mentored' a category of performer. This in itself guaranteed an increased edge. Then add the fact that he hired two argumentative judges to sit alongside him – Louis Walsh and Sharon Osbourne – and the sparks were soon flying. In the run-up to the Series One finale, both Walsh and Osbourne had directed damning words at Cowell's finalist, Steve Brookstein. Then, on the night of the final itself, Osbourne launched an astonishing last-minute attack on both Brookstein and Cowell. Although it was a diatribe that went beyond what Cowell could have wanted, in his eyes the controversy it caused was no bad thing. From there onwards, *The X Factor* has always included a large slice of rivalry on the panel. The following year, Osbourne threw a glass of water over Walsh after he had made a remark about her husband Ozzy during a live show. Cowell's glee as he watched Osbourne's attack was clear to all. With the judges often having the casting vote as to which contestant left the live show each week, there was even more scope for conflict. For instance, Cowell one week accused Walsh of being 'spiteful' for voting off one of his acts.

When her fellow judges were asked how they felt about Dannii being brought on board, there was little sense of the conflict to come. Osbourne said she was 'very excited, but it's exciting to try something new. And Dannii's a little firecracker, there's no floss on her. This series is kind of going into the unknown.'

Walsh, meanwhile, was more measured in his enthusiasm. 'I thought it was strange at the start,' he admitted. 'But I think it's a good thing because we have to work harder. Our reputations are on the line. [Dannii's] been in the business for 27 years and she likes music and she knows what she's doing.'

However, by the time the live shows came around, Dannii was feeling isolated and at odds with Walsh and Osbourne. Dannii increasingly felt under attack from the pair as the live shows progressed. The effect was palpable to those closest to her; even Cowell noticed with some concern that there were tensions and that they were having a bad effect on the Australian. 'She kind of got lost a little bit along the way,' he said looking back at her dark times, but added supportively, 'But I think she does a good job, I really do.'

A good job indeed, but that was not enough to protect her feelings when she felt under attack from her fellow judges. Walsh actually prompted Dannii to storm off the set during one of the live shows after he cattily suggested she could not sing. She had criticised an act for singing out of tune when Louis replied, 'Dannii, singing out of tune? Ho, ho!'

Dannii walked off set and failed to return on time from a commercial break. Osbourne sat on Cowell's lap in Dannii's absence, making a joke out of her discomfort. Walsh had hurt Dannii's feelings but she tried to be philosophical about it, looking at it through his eyes. 'Louis, who's had a rough year after being kicked off the show, then coming back, is thinking, Who is this young chick? What does she know?' she said. 'But to even go there with the arguments is giving power to them, so I ignore it. [Walsh and Osbourne] may rubbish my experience and, OK, I've never had a number one – but I came damn close with a number two [her 2003 hit "I Begin to Wonder"]. I only got beaten by Christina Aguilera's "Beautiful", which is an incredible song. I can't be bothered to retaliate, though.'

Dannii added that she felt she had to tiptoe around Osbourne. She just kept her head down and attempted to focus on mentoring her acts so they could last as long as possible in the show. In this task, she was to be very successful as the line-up for the final would show.

By the time the final came around, the level of tension on the judging panel was sky-high. So much so that the pre-finale press conference proved to be less about the final contestants and more about the rivalries and bitching between the judges. As one newspaper report put it, 'Sharon hates Dannii. Simon fancies Dannii, but Louis picks on her because he loves Sharon. Oh, and Simon's the one who (reluctantly) sacked Louis.'

Nowhere in here was any news about the contestants who would go head to head in the final. This was an aspect of the show that would draw criticism and cause Cowell to wonder whether there was a case for pulling back a bit with the conflict, in order to focus on the talent. During the previous days Osbourne had been letting rip about Dannii to anyone who would listen, implying that the Aussie had been hired by Cowell only because he was attracted to her. It was all good hype, and these sorts of tensions have been a successful feature of Cowell's shows for many years.

During the press conference, Osbourne was asked about her disagreements with Dannii and said, 'It's an even playing field. Dannii speaks about me, I speak about her. It's kind of Round One and Round Two and we're up to round ten now. But it has taken me years to say something nice about Simon Cowell, so I haven't done badly with Dannii, have I?'

However, Dannii was in no mood to be so dismissive of the effects of the rows that had dominated the series. 'It's catty, it's almost become bullying to me, and I don't want to entertain that,' she said. 'I've looked up to Sharon and Louis for years and I wanted to be part of that gang. But, when they're slating you, you think, Please don't, I really like you.'

Naturally, some sceptics wondered whether or not the tensions were genuine or whether they were merely a game that the judges played out onscreen to be replaced by giggles and hugs the moment they were backstage.

However, according to reports, just a few weeks earlier Cowell had called a meeting of the judges to ask them to take control over the growing feuds. 'He told them he didn't mind all the bitchiness and backstabbing while the cameras were rolling, as it made great television, but he wanted it to stop backstage,' said a source close to Cowell. 'He said it was making the rest of the crew uncomfortable and wasn't good for the show. He asked Sharon and Dannii to stop the bitchy comments and for Louis to stop getting involved.'

Certainly, Dannii had become genuinely upset by the controversy. She said that Walsh and Osbourne had been openly derisive of her backstage from the start. 'They came up to me and they said, full on, "You are a young, pretty girl, kind of dumb, you'll just sit there saying, 'Oh, I love everything, aren't you nice.' " ' However, Dannii is no pushover and happily said that sitting next to Osbourne made her 'feel young'.

An enraged Osbourne responded with a vitriolic attack on Dannii during an interview on *The Graham Norton Show*. 'She knows she's there because of her looks, not because of her contribution to the music industry. She's younger, she's better-looking, Simon wants her and he doesn't want me, thank God.'

Osbourne confirmed too that the tension was just as

strong off-camera as it was on-camera. 'It's like a soap opera backstage,' she told Norton. 'I said to Simon yesterday, It's like bloody *Dynasty* now. It's terrible, you know, you have to duck going down the hallway to your dressing room in case there's a little spear that gets you in the back of the neck. You walk in and wonder what the atmosphere is going to be like.'

Next to put his own thoughts into this potent mix was Osbourne's brother David Arden. He alleged that her dislike of Dannii was part of a longstanding issue she had. '[Osbourne] always wants to be Queen Bee and won't let anything stand in her way. Never mind bees, the claws were out and were proving stinging enough in themselves.'

Osbourne is a formidable foe to have, as many entertainment-industry figures have discovered to their cost during her colourful career. Not that she was the only feisty *X Factor* personality who had harsh words to say about Dannii. Cowell's sidekick Sinitta – a longstanding contact and friend of his – was upset by Dannii's appointment too. 'I would definitely be better than Dannii,' said Sinitta. 'I don't think she takes away from the show but I don't think she brings anything new.'

However, on the night of the final, Dannii could leave all this discord behind her and have the last laugh. After all, of the three acts in the final, two of them had been mentored by her. 'It's bloody satisfying to be the only person with two acts left,' she said. 'It just shows that when you focus on your acts, and not on sniping at each other, you get the job done.'

Her pre-eminent position on the night of the final spoke louder than any bitchy words could. Focused and ambitious as ever, Dannii was truly having the last laugh even before a single note had been sung. Her two remaining acts – Leon Jackson and Rhydian Roberts – lined up against the band Same Difference.

She watched proudly as her two acts sang brilliantly on the night. Her efforts with them had clearly paid off. Jackson sang 'White Christmas' and 'You Don't Know Me', but the highlight of his evening and of the entire series came with his duet. It is customary for the finalists to perform a duet with an established, famous act. For Jackson's duet, Dannii had arranged a superstar – and had been able to call in a family favour to secure her. He sang a swing version of 'Better the Devil You Know', and at the end of the first verse introduced Kylie Minogue to the stage. As she appeared, the audience were hysterical with joy. The judges, too, stood up in appreciation. Dannii – wearing a fine red dress – watched proudly as she saw her sister and her *X Factor* act duet. She had described him as 'our very own Braveheart'. Roberts, too, was on form on the night, being joined by Katherine Jenkins for his duet song. However, the highlight for him came during one of the two songs he sang alone. 'I can't even speak, that was so beautiful,' Dannii said proudly, choking back tears after he had sung 'Somewhere'. 'Not only is Rhydian a professional who delivers every week, his heart is as big as his voice and his hair,' she had said before the final.

Well, with his performance of 'Somewhere', his voice was absolutely enormous.

Same Difference trailed behind Jackson and Roberts when the votes were frozen for the first time on the night, and were therefore eliminated first. This guaranteed that Dannii would be the winning judge, whichever of the two remaining acts won the final public vote. In her first series of the show, Dannii had pulled off an unparalleled *X Factor* feat, by mentoring both of the final two artists. Here, she had the last laugh over Osbourne and Walsh. Neither of them had a single act in the final. Indeed, Osbourne had had only one act – Andy Abraham in Series Two – in the final of any of the three series she had participated in. Dannii's pride and joy was immense, and rightly so. Each of her acts sang once more each and then it was time for the winner to be crowned. 'The winner of *The X Factor* 2007 is ...' began Dermot O'Leary, before the traditional pause to build the tension, '... Leon!'

The two finalists embraced as the audience – including Dannii – applauded and cheered. Leon was naturally overjoyed.

'It just means the world ... I love singing,' Leon said. 'I'm really pleased that I've done my country proud, and been the first Scot winner. I've just won a £1 million record deal and I've just changed me and my mum's life for ever.

'I'm stunned, absolutely stunned. My birthday's just after Christmas, and this is probably the best birthday and Christmas present I've had in my whole life.'

Jackson's joy was matched in its intensity by the surprise at his victory that was felt in many corners. Many viewers had expected Roberts to win and were extremely surprised when that was not the case. Even the bookmakers were taken aback. Ladbrokes spokesman Nick Weinberg said, 'Leon's win is the biggest shock in the history of reality TV betting.'

Roberts was graceful on the night, although his father Malcolm said, he was 'disappointed for himself and his fans'. As for Dannii, she could bask in the glory of having been the mentor of the winner *and* the runner-up. It had certainly been an impressive start to her *X Factor* career. After the final, Cowell was full in his praise for the new judge. 'She's worked harder with the artists than anyone else. She did 20-hour days,' he said.

Jackson himself praised her, too, and he lifted the lid on the simplicity of her mentoring approach, explaining that she had offered some specific advice but ultimately told him, 'Just be yourself, enjoy every minute of it and don't take yourself too seriously.'

She recalled that it was during the judges'-houses stage of the competition that she first noticed the winning qualities in Jackson. 'It was funny because, when we were in Ibiza, I heard a special quality in Leon's voice and I really wanted to give him a go, and I said to him, "If you don't believe in yourself, just remember I

believe in you, so just get up there and give it a shot," '
she said. 'The only time Leon ever faltered with his
vocals was when he was not sure about himself, and
that's understandable under the pressure. The minute he
took hold of the reins and went, "Yeah! This is my shot
at it", you couldn't fault him.'

Jackson too recalled his experiences with Dannii in
the judges'-houses phase with fondness. 'We stayed at
this amazing place overlooking the sea. It was
breathtaking. During our singing sessions, we were by
the pool and had a live guitarist and pianist. I sat not far
from Dannii and was just singing to her. I really just let
go and enjoyed myself.'

Another contestant who speaks highly of Dannii is
Luke Bayer. He entered the series in Dannii's first year and
got as far as the Ibiza phase of her group, but lost out in
favour or Jackson, Roberts and Williams. Dannii felt that
Bayer was too young to go through to the live shows. He
was a memorable contestant, though. He had a fine voice
and a loveable personality, and his intense emotions
throughout the competition won him many admirers.
Looking back on his encounter with her, he is full of
admiration for Dannii. 'She was very gorgeous. On
initially meeting her I thought, Wow, she's stunning,' he
recalls with a smile. 'She's very small, which is cute. She's
lovely. Very small, very pretty. She's got very nice eyes.' He
was delighted when her casting vote put him through the
initial audition phase. 'As a singer, she actually knows
what she's on about, so it meant a lot,' he said.

He and his fellow male contestants were delighted when they discovered that Dannii was to be their mentor for the latter stages of the competition. 'We didn't know anything,' he confirms of the day when they waited to discover which of the four judges had been assigned to their category. 'The door to the room we were waiting in kept opening and closing, opening and closing. They were testing our reactions. Then she came through and we were so excited! Because we were her first year and also because she's so stunning we were like: We've got the hot judge.'

Once they had flown to Ibiza, they met Dannii, who gave Bayer and his fellow contestants a pep talk. 'She wished us all the best of luck and explained that she'd be judging us on that performance and that performance only,' he said. 'It was going to be a clean slate, which lessened the pressure on us.'

Once it came to the time where she broke the news to Bayer that she was not taking him to the live shows, he was devastated, but also admired how she handled the moment. 'I thought she was very good at it, actually,' he says. 'With me being young at the time she was very gentle with me. It wasn't shown on camera but she came up to me afterwards to check I was OK. She was really lovely and went into her reasoning as to why she didn't put me through. She didn't need to do that, so that shows how genuine she was. She started off young, so I think she knew how I'd be feeling. She was very nice about it all and she looked genuinely upset when she had to turn me away. I'm sure it was difficult for her.'

For all the boys in the Ibiza stage, Dannii had prepared a gift to show them how much she appreciated their efforts and valued their talent. 'She brought us all T-shirts saying Team Minogue and gave each of us a note saying well done for getting so far and how much she appreciated our hard work,' recalls Bayer. He then watched as Dannii took two of her three acts all the way to the final, with Jackson triumphing. 'I wasn't surprised she did so well at all,' said Bayer. 'She had planned it all out all along. Before I went to Ibiza, she changed my songs a few times. She wanted to bring the best out of people and she made numerous changes to the song choices for people.' She had arranged tickets to the live shows for Bayer and he was touched that she went out of her way to welcome him and offer further encouragement. 'In one of the breaks she got up – she was wearing a very short blue dress I remember – and when she saw me she said, "Oh my God, Luke!" and ran up to me and gave me a big hug,' he says. 'She was lovely, really, really nice. It was just her being herself.'

Given that Dannii has a reputation among some as something of an ice queen, did Bayer himself notice any of that in her? 'I think she maybe stands off a bit at the beginning while she works you out, but she is lovely, she is lovely,' he insists. 'She likes honest people, that was my impression. She appreciated it when Rhydian went back to the live shows and told her how he thought she was doing.' Bayer also noted that she is a deep thinker who considers her every move before acting. 'I think she thinks into things an awful lot, like how what she does will affect people. She's a big thinker. That's really good, I think. She was right: at the time I wasn't ready for it. I think she'd have loved to put me through but she was thinking about the effect that would have on me. I think in the long run she was right, and it was better for me to not go through.'

Dannii's fine showing in the final helped her shrug off some of the unpleasant things that had been said about her during the series. For instance, she was dismissive of the rumours that she and Cowell were a romantic item, even brushing aside a much-reproduced photograph of them looking cosy in the back of a car. 'Simon and I do flirt in a really fun way and I'm pretty tactile,' she admitted. 'We click and get on really well. But that man could flirt with a book, a wall, anything. That picture looked so wrong but it wasn't at all – we weren't even holding hands. Simon was just stretching out his arms.'

She continued, explaining which sort of men did tickle her fancy, as well as those who do not. 'I don't fancy him and I don't have a type I go for, but I like a man who makes me laugh, who's intelligent and speaks his mind. Maybe I should go for a chef, because an ideal date for me would have to involve food. Gordon Ramsay's sexy. I met him at the *GQ* Awards and thought, Yeah, you're lovely. I haven't met Marco Pierre White but my friends adore him. You could never be with a guy like that, he's too outrageous, but it doesn't stop you liking him. Marco and Gordon are proper men's men. I need someone to sweep me off my feet, a knight in shining armour to give me a fairytale romance.'

All the same, the Cowell rumour was too much for some sections of the press to give up on immediately. It continued to be thrown at her. Asked the same question in a separate newspaper interview, she again dismissed the suggestion. 'Simon's lovely, but no, not true,' she laughed. 'I think he felt a bit sorry for me. And yes, he would hold my arm when we walked down the steps, but that was because I was wearing a long dress and high heels and I was terrified of falling! And, anyway, have you seen his girlfriend? She's gorgeous!'

However, the shadow cast by her clashes with Osbourne remained over the proceedings. Even after the series was finished, whispers in the press still cast Dannii as the baddy. 'Sharon wasn't jealous because Dannii was a glamorous woman,' said an unnamed friend of Osbourne. 'She could have coped if she respected her if it was Myleene Klass or Mel B, for example, but she didn't think Dannii had any musical credibility. She thought everything she said was clichéd and boring. They were like oil and water.'

The same 'friend' dismissed the success Dannii had been on the programme. 'Dannii won last year because she had the easiest category. Simon also gave Dannii all the attention. It was obvious he was enamoured with her.'

When Dannii learned that Osbourne had quit the show, there was no official comment from her but an aide said, 'She is genuinely shocked by Sharon's decision and hopes it has nothing to do with her.'

Even Walsh continued the bitchiness after the series had ended, dubbing Dannii and Cowell 'Sonny and Cher' and making unfavourable comparisons between Dannii and her sister. 'I've been real,' he said. 'I haven't acted … unlike some people, Dannii! There are kind of two camps – Dannii and Simon and me and Sharon. Sharon and I call them Sonny and Cher, and we're Richard and Judy. We haven't all been out together the whole series and the dynamic has changed. I've been out with Sharon occasionally, but that's it. Sharon's a friend. I like her because she keeps it real. I don't think the public are behind Dannii in the same way they are Kylie. With the right producers, she could have had a number one with "Touch Me Like That" but instead she only got to number 43 in the midweek chart.'

As Dannii might have reflected, the X Factor acts she had mentored all the way to the final were certainly being warmed to by the public, and both enjoyed top-five hits off the back of the show. Having had the last laugh on her first series on The X Factor, Dannii then had another cause for happiness when she signed up for the next series, for which she would receive a reported fee of £900,000.

With Osbourne gone, at least she had seen the back of her old adversary. However, Osbourne's replacement was Girls Aloud singer Cheryl Cole, and the media sensed potential for a new feud. The narrative was predictable: Osbourne had been put out when a younger prettier judge (Minogue) had joined the panel, therefore Minogue would be put out when a younger prettier judge (Cole) joined the panel. It was an unimaginative and inherently misogynistic theory. That said, Dannii and Girls Aloud had form and during a war of words in 2005 she had dismissed the members of the band saying, 'I'm no chav!'

Dannii subsequently admitted, 'It's true that Girls Aloud have said some unfortunate things about me, but you can't hold onto things like that. I barely know Cheryl yet. We've been so busy we've not spent much time together, but she brings an important new angle to the show. I'm pop and she's urban. It's a great mix. When we do get to spend time together, I hope we get on. I don't ever want to go through the same atmosphere as before.'

She spoke openly of the hurt she had felt during the previous year's competition. 'For some reason, Sharon did not like me. I don't know what I did to upset her, and on several occasions I went to her to try to sort things out. But she kept slagging me off. I was devastated when she laid into me. It was awful. I don't understand her. But then I don't understand a woman who throws off her shoes and runs off midway through a live TV show. It's not the sort of behaviour I've ever been exposed to before. My response was-to just focus on my artists and win the show.' Looking back now, Dannii says she respects much of what Osbourne has achieved in her life but does not always respect the way she behaves. 'And I always wanted to meet Ozzy Osbourne, but I guess that's out of the question now,' she jokes.

With the new instalment of the competition under way, Dannii denied there was any problem between her and her new fellow judge. 'Anything that's been said about us not getting on has not come from us,' she insisted as the rumours rose. 'Cheryl's been positive since she joined the show, and so have I. There's just nothing there. We're still getting to know each other. We don't socialise outside work but I don't socialise with any of the judges. It does take a while to get to know each other and obviously I've had longer with Louis and Simon, but by the end of show Cheryl and I will know each other better. And I love the fact she doesn't take any nonsense from Simon and just gets in there and does the job and is not afraid to have her own opinion. She's been amazing since Day One.'

However, an insider painted a less harmonious portrait of proceedings in the *Mirror*. 'Dannii walked into Arsenal's Emirates Stadium for the auditions and you could tell she'd put in a lot of work into looking good. She knows there's a younger, more successful, more attractive kid on the block and they will both be fighting for attention. She's 36 and Cheryl is just 24 and she's desperate not to be cast as the older Sharon

Osbourne type – she wants to be Cheryl's equal. But it isn't working out like that.'

The same insider was quick to praise Cole – to the detriment of Dannii. '[Cole] has a great empathy for those auditioning because she has been there herself. She has had a tough time and knows what it is like to go through this process. Simon is delighted with how things have gone. He is calling her the "new Cilla Black". She has that touch that connects with people. She is a natural fit to the show and makes Dannii somewhat redundant. Louis and Cheryl get on like a house on fire as he managed Girls Aloud. He has never really got on with Dannii, so that has made her feel even more isolated. It's ironic that last year Sharon felt under threat from the younger rival when Dannii arrived. Now it is Dannii, who is under pressure herself.'

Cole, though, has since denied the entire story, saying that it is not only untrue but also based on misogynistic stereotype. 'It's as if, because you are both women, you must hate each other,' she said. 'They did it last year with Sharon [Osbourne] and Dannii because Sharon was older, and now they're going on about the age thing with Dannii and me. It is a stupid stereotype which is not true.'

Kylie, too, has blasted the same rumours saying they are 'so cheap'. All the same, Dannii was praised by many for managing to compete with the glamorous and gorgeous Cole. 'Few women could stand alongside Cheryl Cole and still look stunning,' chimed the *Mirror*, 'but Dannii pulls it off.' At least some of the commentary was going Dannii's way.

She admitted, though, that times had been tough for her the previous year on *The X Factor* as Osbourne struggled to adapt to her presence. 'I'd watched the show as a fan and was so excited to be taking part, then to think that just by being there I was causing unhappiness was awful, really awful,' she said. 'It would be same for anyone: "I really, really want to be here." Then you think, Oh, I'm upsetting people. That was the awful bit. In the end I had to just get on with it, turn up and do my job. I think a certain amount of people wanted the Dannii–Sharon spat to continue with me and Cheryl. But I keep saying to people, "Unless you get Sharon back it's just not going to happen! Stop dreaming." All I know is I love the show and I don't like any hard feelings with anyone. I'm very eager to make the workplace a happy place.'

Well, eager to a point. She was not so eager that she could resist returning some of the jibes made by Louis Walsh in the media. Walsh had suggested that Osbourne could be on her way back to *The X Factor* to replace Dannii. 'Naughty little leprechaun,' she said. 'I tell him that's the only way he can get on TV. He can't help but stir things up, but he admits that.'

In the next series, she would once again clash with Walsh, this time even more memorably. Her response was devastatingly moving. During the live finals there was a Take That-themed week. Walsh claimed he had earmarked the song 'Rule the World' for his act JLS, but Dannii claimed it for her act Rachel Hylton. The two judges clashed over who should have had the song, with Walsh snapping, 'We're all in it for our acts. We all care and I have to protect my acts as well.'

The judges work to a rota for first dibs over song choice week by week, which Dannii reminded Walsh of. However, the Irishman was in no mood to back down. 'But they wanted to do "Rule the World" from Day One,' he said of his band JLS.

Dannii became increasingly exasperated and upset. She was soon in tears. Cowell, realising that the situation was becoming increasingly tense, said, 'You two need to kiss and make up.'

Walsh then leaned over to kiss Dannii, whose body language remained hostile.

Later in the show, Cowell came to Dannii's defence, saying, 'Just picking up on what Louis said about nicking the song, we take it in turns and Dannii made absolutely the right decision, and if Louis doesn't like it … tough.'

She was pleased to have Cowell's support, not least because there had been a tense moment between her and the boss just weeks earlier. During some inter-judge banter, Dannii had reclaimed the credit for the previous year's winner Jackson, at the expense of Cowell. 'Simon did not discover Leon,' she said. 'He didn't even want him in the competition.'

For Cowell, this remark went over the line and he

would sternly remind Dannii not to repeat such talk. They moved on from that moment quickly but her latest clash with Walsh cut more deeply. 'I'm not made of steel,' she said. 'It got heated on- and off-set, and there's only so many times I can be pushed around.' For her, Walsh's claim that she had effectively stolen the song from his act was an unjustified attack. 'It got to the point where I had to defend my character. I'm sure the audience were eating it up, but it's different when you're actually in that seat. It was absolutely horrible. I would never want to go through that again, or see anyone else go through it. But it's what you sign up for.' She admits, looking back, that the whole episode seems silly, 'but at the time it was just a build-up of everything. I just felt that my character is so much about what's right or wrong. Saying something that isn't true and that I wouldn't do is big.'

Once more she was left feeling peculiarly isolated, Cowell's support notwithstanding. For further comfort, she turned to an unlikely ally – the online media. 'I went on a couple of the online polls to see what was going on – 99.9 per cent of the people were saying, "This is utter crap", and I thought, OK, now I can put it in perspective.'

She was to be voted as *OK!* magazine readers' favourite *X Factor* judge for the series, too. The *OK!* contest saw 48 per cent choose her, while Cole finished second with 37 per cent of the vote, followed by Cowell with 12 per cent and Walsh with just 3 per cent.

Walsh was to face even more uncomfortable reading when Kylie came out in support of her Dannii. 'I'm so proud of my sister and it annoys the hell out of me when comparisons between us are made,' she said. 'In England you lot don't know where she came from. She was on TV every week from seven years old. It makes it harder for her when she gets Louis Walsh's rather pathetic jibes, one of which is she hasn't had a hit record, and that's just not true.'

She had been handed the traditionally difficult Over-25s category for this series and none of her acts lasted until the semifinals of the live shows. That said, she had kept the category intact until Week Six of the live rounds, which was a new record for the category. 'It wasn't a bad run,' said Dannii. 'It's the longest the Over-25s have stayed in the competition.'

And, again, she had faced jibes, with Irish comedian Graham Norton saying that Dannii was a bad mentor to have. 'She's like tying a lump of concrete around your neck,' said Norton, a strange sentiment to express given that in the previous series Dannii had mentored both of the top two acts, setting a new record. But Walsh came out in support of Dannii, saying, 'Don't give her a hard time.'

By the time the 2009 series came around, Walsh was in even more conciliatory mood. On the first day of filming, he strode up to Dannii and said, 'I'm so sorry, please don't let me do that again.'

She had stipulated that her continued involvement

with *The X Factor* was dependent on a cessation of hostilities. 'Last year it was clear to everyone that I wasn't having fun,' she said of the 2008 series, 'and I made it very clear that, if it was going to be anything like that again, then I didn't want to go there.' She also reportedly demanded – and received – a £250,000 pay rise, which took her fee for the series to £1 million.

Her newfound closeness to Walsh was evident when the Irishman struggled to adjust to the new format, in which the opening auditions are held in front of a live arena audience. 'Louis was freaking out. I had to keep giving him cuddles to calm him down,' she says. 'Even though he's done the live shows, that's not his comfort zone. Whereas it's great for Cheryl and I, and Simon obviously loves an audience.' She later added that she had seen 'a different side' to Walsh this time round.

She was enjoying this series of *The X Factor* more than ever. The public, too, were warming to her as never before. She had not entirely seen off the doubters, but when asked what her qualifications were for a place on the panel she answered firmly. 'What does qualify someone for this job – 30 years in the music business; television, theatre, film?' she asked pointedly. 'Surviving it without running off the rails like a lot of other people? You know, maybe I do have some of the skills to do it.'

Dannii was to perform well in the 2009 series, taking one of her acts – the wonderful Stacey Solomon – all the way to the final weekend. 'I am absolutely in love with that girl,' said Dannii of Solomon. Discerning viewers felt exactly the same.

Along the way, Dannii inadvertently stepped into a major controversy during her response to Cowell's act, 28-year-old teacher Danyl Johnson. Johnson had almost brought the house down with his rendition of 'And I'm Telling You' from the musical *Dreamgirls* – originally sung by Jennifer Hudson. Johnson had altered the lyrics to make the song pertinent to his gender, and Dannii was to refer to this in her verdict. 'It was a fantastic performance, a true *X Factor* performance – turning guys into girls,' she said. But then she added, 'No need to change the gender references, if we're to believe everything we read in the press,' in reference to Johnson's revelation in the *News of the World* that he is bisexual.

Cowell angrily asked her what she had said, and she repeated the point. Johnson could be seen mouthing, 'I'm not ashamed' to the audience. When it came to Cowell's verdict, the atmosphere became even more tense. 'I think we're missing something here. I just heard one of the best performances I ever heard in my life,' he said. The audience erupted with joy and Johnson seemed close to tears. Cowell had not finished, though. He turned to Dannii and stormed, 'And you can forget playing any of those games with him. I'm not having that. This guy sang his heart out. Give him some credit.'

In the wake of the show, Dannii came under astonishing attack for her joke. The official *X Factor* website was besieged with angry comments. 'Dannii's comments were disrespectful and out of order!' wrote one fan. 'Danyl's sexual orientation was under siege when tonight's show should have been about the music.'

Another echoed the sentiment saying, 'I sat here shocked at her comment, which has got to be one of the worst things said on TV.'

The controversy was surprising because Johnson's bisexuality was not secret. He had told the *News of the World*, 'I am a massive flirt. I wouldn't rule out someone just because of their gender.'

Given Dannii's longstanding support for gay and bisexual people, it was shocking to see it suggested that she was in some way acting in a hostile way to Johnson because of his sexuality. However, with *The X Factor* the stakes are always hyped so high that this storm was showing every sign of getting out of all proportion. At 1.35am the following day, she published an online statement about the growing controversy. 'Dannii made a joke about the lyrics of Danyl's song, referencing a recent newspaper interview he has given about his private life. She spoke to Danyl straight after the show, explained what she was talking about and he wasn't offended in the slightest. Dannii is mortified if her comments have been misinterpreted as she has always been hugely supportive of the gay and bisexual community for her entire career.'

Surprisingly, this was not enough for some and media watchdog Ofcom received nearly 4,000 complaints about Dannii's quip in the following days. She then tried again to calm the storm with a fresh statement. 'It was meant to be a humorous moment about the fact he had an opportunity to have fun with his song. Danyl and I were joking about the very same thing in rehearsals on Friday, so it carried on to the show. I'd like to apologise to anyone that was offended by my comments, it was never my intention,' said Dannii, whose job was reportedly in doubt as a result of the controversy. 'I spoke to Danyl straight after the show and he wasn't offended or upset by my comments, and knew exactly what I was saying.'

Johnson accepted Minogue's apology and insisted, 'I was not at all offended by Dannii's comment. We're completely cool about it and chatted after the show.'

The competition has become more and more intense with each series and this is something that all involved keenly feel. 'I personally get very wrapped up with the contestants,' said Dannii, 'wanting to know if they feel OK.' She added, 'I don't think you can be aware that half the country's watching, otherwise you would completely freeze up.' Asked if she felt the pressure that is heaped on her and Cheryl Cole to come up with a dazzling new look each show, she said she did. She admitted that she was pleased when the verdict of the press after a show was that she had looked better than Cole. 'You give it a little F1: "Yes" ' she said. 'I spent so many years reading headlines that I was the fat, ugly sister that you kind of do get a little bit of joy out of thinking you looked good. Every girl likes that.'

The host of *The X Factor*'s sister show, *The Xtra Factor*, Holly Willoughby, has enjoyed watching Dannii flourish. 'I think the British public have been able to get to know somebody who before they just didn't get the chance to know.'

But a hint of how deeply the argument with Walsh about Take That might have hurt her came when she responded negatively to a compliment Cowell had made about her. Singing her praises, he said, 'Dannii works harder than all of us. She's so obsessive about winning, and I like that.'

As we have seen, Cowell has always admired competitiveness and ambition too, so it was clearly a compliment. But, when a newspaper interviewer reminded her of this quote, she was not entirely happy with the sentiment Cowell ascribed to her. 'I'm obsessive, but not about winning,' she said, perhaps mindful of the accusation that she had stolen a Take That song the previous year. 'I'm obsessive about looking after the acts. I've been performing from a really young age, so I really want them to have a good time. It's a lot of pressure and I want to make sure that they're all fine.'

And there was no doubt that Cowell's respect and personal affection towards her was strong as a result of their working together for three years. In July 2009, his ex-girlfriend and longstanding friend Jackie St Claire threw a surprise birthday party, ahead of his official party later in the year. It was actually *her* birthday but somehow the guests thought the festivities were also to recognise Cowell's birthday, so it turned into a double-celebration. During the bash, Dannii, Amanda Holden and St Claire belted out the Carly Simon hit 'You're So Vain' to Cowell, with Louis Walsh and choreographer Bruno Tonioli on backing vocals. No wonder that Cowell stood open-mouthed as he watched the performance. An onlooker said, '[St Claire] knew the performance would really make him laugh. Dannii took the lead vocals and the others came out providing the comedy for the show. Simon was in a fit of giggles throughout – especially when Louis joined in and minced along to the words.' The source added that Cowell took it in good humour: 'Simon *is* so vain but, unlike some, he is the first to admit it. So it was the perfect joke.'

The following month one of Dannii's co-vocalists for that performance, Amanda Holden, wrote in her *News of the World* column that on the night of the St Claire-arranged bash she had copied an outfit, having previously seen Dannii pull it off so well. 'The dress code for tonight is "heavenly white", so I'm wearing a Yeojin Bae gown I saw Dannii Minogue wear a few years ago,' she wrote. 'Rena Zhang, the dress designer, very kindly cut a thigh-high slit in it. I bump into Dannii tonight and admit: "I'm a stalker when it comes to you and fashion." She notices the split and tells me she covers her legs since a magazine reported it looks like her knees have little faces on!'

Dannii will no doubt have enjoyed seeing such a

glamorous and successful woman as Holden – who judges alongside Cowell on *Britain's Got Talent* – following a trend she had set.

Thanks to her starring role in successive series of *Australia's Got Talent* and *The X Factor*, Dannii's fame in both Australia and Britain was sky high. With her career very much in a strong position, the only thing that needed to be added to the picture was renewed personal happiness. Thanks to a younger man she had recently met, Dannii was indeed happier than ever.

CHAPTER EIGHT

mum's the word

Much has been made of Dannii's use of Botox. Like many celebrities, she has never attempted to hide her use of the anti-ageing treatment. However, in Dannii's case, one can almost chart her emotional state by whether she is using it or not. She blamed her sister's cancer, together with other stresses of her life at the time, for persuading her to use Botox in the first place. She has always been honest and realistic about her use of it, and clear about the reasons why. 'I've always been very conscious of my health and appearance – because, with my job, I'm constantly under the microscope. My sister was sick, then my best friend died soon after – I felt I'd been hit by a wave,' she said. 'I couldn't deal with the stress. I couldn't deal with having to look at my face. It was a personal thing of having to get through a lot of sadness. At first, it was something fun I tried, then it became a necessity.' However, since meeting the man who was to become the father of her first child, she said she was so happy that she was no longer drawn to using Botox. Dannii said, 'I don't need Botox now and don't want it. Life is just so different now. I'm in such an incredible place. I guess at my age I have to start thinking about babies at some time. But, to be honest, I'm just enjoying being so wildly in love and being so happy. He is the one.' She was similarly gleeful about her new man during a chat with the *Mirror*. She said, 'I've never been happier. I am just so, so in love. For the first year, we've been working out how to be together because our jobs are so crazy and all over the place. But I know he's The One.'

So who was this man who was being declared 'The One' by Dannii? Kris Smith has played for leading rugby-league clubs Leeds and Halifax. Her fondness for the rugby player look was longstanding. When asked what she would do if she could become invisible for a day, she said, 'Go on the set of the shoot for the French rugby team's next calendar.'

The 6ft 4in hunk has been described as 'a man mountain' by the *Sun*. She first met him in Ibiza in 2008. As Smith revealed, she first wondered if he was a ladies' man at all. 'She was discussing with her friends if I was gay or not,' said Kris. 'Now we're together so I can prove a point – I'm not gay.' As for him, he did not at first recognise her. 'When I first started speaking to her, I had no idea who she was,' he told an Australian radio station. 'It was only afterwards when a friend told me.'

When he did realise who she was, it was said that he delighted by his good fortune. 'He can't believe his luck and has been showing off photos of him and Dannii together on dates,' a friend told the *Daily Star*. 'Kris is a big lad who's in great shape physically. He's just been bowled over by Dannii's interest in him. He wants to make it work.'

She said that, despite how well things were going with Smith, she had no inclination to start a family with him just yet. 'I'm godmother to two of my friends' children and, that's enough for me right now. I've seen how hard it is. Way too hard. I guess I should start thinking about it soon. but I still feel so young – surely I can't be old enough to have kids. I'm too irresponsible for that! I think with a lot of women now if you're not settled you just think, I want to wait, there's no point rushing things. It's way too much for me now and the thought of it frightens me. I'd want to be in a really stable relationship before I even thought about having kids. It takes time to be with someone and I'm just not at that point where I'm thinking about it. A lot of people are keen to do it on their own but it's just not an option for me. I'm really old-fashioned. I've had such a great upbringing, my parents have been fab; they're together and still madly in love. I just wouldn't want to do it on my own.'

Dannii had first publicly confirmed the relationship when she wrote in her *Closer* magazine column,

'Rumours are flying about my new-found interest in the Rugby League, and the papers say I'm dating an ex-Leeds player. Hmm, what can I tell you? Well, I currently don't know anything about the game but there's a good reason to start learning!' With a tiny bit less coyness, she added, 'Let's put it this way, Cupid had asked for his arrow back! I'm not one to reveal much about my love life but I'm a happy girl.'

A few weeks later, the *News of the World* claimed the world exclusive on a photograph of the happy couple. Saying that Smith had 'put the smile back on her face after a year-long sex drought', it featured them on holiday together. She enjoyed showing Smith around Australia, she said. 'It's been so nice to share him with my family and show him Australia for the first time,' she told the *Mirror*. 'I've never been to central Australia and would love to go there,' she said. 'We will do the very touristy thing of going to the Australia Zoo too. It's good because [with] all these things I will be as much a tourist as he will be. He has been talking to his friends back in Manchester and it's minus five. He loves it here.'

Only weeks earlier, she had admitted that she was 'picky' when it came to men, and a new serious relationship had consequently seemed a long way off for her. 'It's too easy to say that successful, independent women are single because they focus too much on their work,' she said. 'If the right guy came along, I'd be happy, but I'm picky. And not everybody has to get married and have children to be happy.' Since meeting

Smith, though, she was becoming increasingly willing to go down precisely that road. All the same, for Smith his relationship with Dannii meant he had to adjust to a sudden surge in interest in his private life. Adjusting to this was part of the life Smith had chosen when hooking up with Dannii. He did well to adjust to it, and they seemed gleefully happy in the early stages of their love.

However, just four months into the relationship, it was claimed that the couple had split. Dannii, it was reported, had called time on Smith after they argued constantly. 'She is upset but says she has done the right thing by ending her relationship,' a friend reportedly told the *Mirror*. 'She's [spent] a lot of time looking after her [*X Factor*] contestant Ruth Lorenzo and then trying to get on with her fellow judges. The last thing she needs is to be stressed by a relationship.' Next up for her, it was said, was a break and then a new start with a clean slate. 'She hopes to have a long holiday to recharge her batteries, and she may return to Oz to spend time with her family,' said the friend.

Having endured some groaning puns around motoring words during her relationship with Villeneuve, Dannii now faced similar wordplay around Smith's sport. 'Dannii kicks lover into touch', was the headline in the *Herald Sun*. Within days, though, this suggestion was flatly denied. Another friend was quoted in the *News of the World* and insisted that Dannii had given them a much different progress report on the matter. The friend claimed that Dannii had told her, 'Kris is my rock. He's been the one thing I can count on this year and the only person who can properly make me smile at the moment.' The source also hinted that, far from being ready to split, the couple were in fact close to being ready to take the relationship to a whole new level. 'Dannii loves Kris to bits and is pretty confident he's the man of her dreams. Marriage is definitely the topic of conversation at the moment.'

When Piers Morgan asked her what the chances of this were, she replied that Smith would need to ask her first. Morgan asked what her answer would be. 'I'd want him to be the first person to hear the answer,' she said. In a separate interview she was cooler about the idea, saying, 'Marriage really scares me.'

In December 2008, with *X Factor* duties behind her for another year, Dannii flew back to Australia with Smith in tow. It was time for him to properly meet her parents. They arrived one Thursday night – on different flights – and were collected at Melbourne Airport by her father Ron. She could bask in the news that, back in Britain, she had been voted Celebrity of the Year. The introduction of Smith to her family over Christmas was a real success, and one reporter was told early in 2009, 'Kris became part of the Minogue family over Christmas and Kylie loved him.'

In the New Year, they were spotted at the Icebergs Dining Room and Bar in Sydney, and their love was obvious to all onlookers, who noted that Dannii could not stop gazing at Smith. She might not be alone in gazing adoringly at her man, for he now has a promising career as a model. In 2009, Smith was revealed as the new face of Australian superstore Myer. 'I'm still learning every day about the timing of the walking, the expression that the choreographer wants from you.' He had modelled only once before but was signed up for the catwalk wearing the store's spring and summer collections. Dannii arranged to be there to watch the Sydney show despite her presence being tricky to arrange. 'It took a month of planning and I'm so jet-lagged I don't even know where I am but I made it,' she said on arrival. She was so excited and proud that she beamed: 'I may just run onto the stage and jump him.'

Reports suggested that her ex-husband Julian McMahon had been due to be at the event but had pulled out when he learned of Dannii's presence. Smith, though, looked just the part as he worked the walkways and he managed to avoid any slip-ups.

His success as a model in Australia led to inevitable discussion over whether the couple would ultimately relocate there. With a six-month modelling contract requiring him to spend that period in Dannii's hometown of Melbourne, it seemed eminently possible that the couple would relocate there. Once again, her 'X Factor future' was therefore cast into doubt. 'We're still not sure what Dannii is doing in terms of X Factor,' said Smith.

Ahead of them starting work, they were due in the UK for a holiday, but what would happen next for them once Smith returned Down Under for his modelling work? As for Smith, he knew what his preference was. 'I would love it if [Dannii] could come back with me and she would love it too,' he said.

Dannii herself restated her love of life in Melbourne when she said of the city, 'It's a lot easier for her to relax here.' In the light of all this, rumours were rife that there would be a possible departure from *The X Factor* by Dannii. 'It was tough for Dannii last year and she got a lot of negative press,' a source told the *Sun*. 'A person can only take so much before asking, "Is it really worth it?" Dannii felt bullied by Sharon during her first series and that was tough, so she was looking forward to Cheryl joining the team last year.' The source added: 'But that became a nightmare too when the rumour mill went into overdrive with stories about the two of them competing against each other for Simon Cowell's attention.'

However, Cowell remained supportive of Dannii. 'If I was a betting man, my money would be on Dannii returning to the show,' he said. 'She was great last year and I am adamant that she should be there for the next series. All being well, pen will be put to paper this week. Despite all the fuss concerning Dannii and Cheryl, I think the four judges worked really well together and gelled. There was an excellent chemistry.' According to reports, he was putting his money where his mouth was, too. An *X Factor* source told the *Mirror*, 'She feels she has been a bit redundant but Simon pleaded with her to stay and has offered her a much more lucrative deal, doubling her £500,000 fees to £1 million.'

Still, Smith was making increasingly positive noises about the couple's love of Melbourne. 'It feels like home [here],' he told the *Herald Sun*. 'It's somewhere I could think about living.' In October 2009, Smith showed his highly romantic and imaginative nature when he secretly arranged to be on a flight that Dannii was taking from Australia. 'They had an emotional goodbye at Minogue Towers and Dannii made her way to the airport,' a source said. 'As she did, Kris quickly packed up a suitcase and got a friend to drive him to the airport and checked in on the same flight and made secret arrangements to be sat next to her. After Dannii got on the plane, Kris went up to her and said, "A glass of champagne for you?" She just screamed! Kris was returning the favour to his girl after she gave him a similar surprise earlier in the summer in Australia.'

The following month, Dannii painted a slightly less idyllic portrait of the relationship during an interview with *Bang Showbiz*. Smith was clearly very hot on the idea of their having children together but Dannii was less than convinced. 'He's very keen to be a dad and I'm taking some convincing,' she said. 'I said, "If you can have the baby then fine." If he does everything, basically, then maybe.' All the same, she was full of joy and said she believed that joy was giving her physical as well as emotional benefits. She said of her relationship with Smith, 'When you're having a good time both at work

and in your love life, I guess it shows on your face ...
I'm amazed at my own good fortune, and so grateful for
it. I feel euphoric.'

At this stage, motherhood for Dannii seemed a long
way off. She was simply happy with how things were
and was enjoying how great she was looking physically
as a result of her emotional wellbeing. So, when
rumours began to circulate that she was expecting a
baby, some observers were a little surprised.

As the whispers grew, there were at first some
denials from the Dannii camp. The *Daily Mail* claimed
she had visited a Melbourne hospital to undergo a
medical exam that identifies health risks in unborn
babies, such as Down's syndrome. But Dannii's agent
Melissa Le Gear insisted the speculation was
'completely inaccurate', adding, 'Reports that said she
was seen in hospital having a particular type of test are
absolutely untrue.'

At this stage, Dannii had not yet reached the 12-week
pregnancy stage, but once she had passed that milestone
she was ready to share the news with the public, and it
was a very 21st-century announcement. Dannii chose to
reveal the news via her Twitter feed. 'Woo hoo I'm going
to be a mummy!' she told her followers.

Kris tweeted on his own Twitter feed, 'Woo hoo I'm
going to be a daddy!'

To complete the online celebration, Kylie too
tweeted about Dannii's big news. 'Congratulations to
my sister Dannii and her partner Kris on the happy

news!!!! I am so excited to be an Aunty again!! WOW
WOW WOW!! xxx'

Her spokesperson delivered the news on the same day
in a more traditional announcement. 'Dannii and Kris
are very excited and can't wait to start their family in
2010. Rumours and stories surfaced across the weekend
about Dannii being pregnant and having already had her
12-week scan. These stories were incorrect. Dannii had
her 12-week scan this week and was given the results
today with the all-clear to make an announcement.'

Dannii and Kris headed to Melbourne's posh Press
Club restaurant to celebrate the news. Opened in 2006,
the Press Club boasts impressive views of some of the
city's most stunning architecture. It is a classy place with
a celebrated cocktail list, but on the day Dannii stuck to
water. In retrospect, the hints had been coming for some
time that Dannii was ready to start a family. In 2009,
during her frank interview with Piers Morgan on ITV,
she said, 'I've never been maternal. I almost thought I
was going to escape it, and now I'm in a relationship
that is just so right, maybe I have to think about it.'

Once thinking had led to an actual pregnancy, the
world was delighted to hear of it. She was warmly
lauded by her fellow X Factor judges. 'Congratulations,'
Simon Cowell told her. 'I'm thrilled for you.'

Meanwhile, Cheryl Cole said, 'I am absolutely thrilled
for Dannii and Kris. I think it's fantastic news and the most
special thing that could have happened to them both.'

Louis Walsh too was pleased, and said, 'It's

tremendous news and a great way for them to start a new decade.'

Naturally, as the speculation over whether she was pregnant ended, discussion turned instead to what effect this would have on her career. Would the ever-ambitious Dannii drop everything in order to be a full-time mother? In recent times, thanks to the manipulative genius of Simon Cowell, there is a constant question mark hovering over the future of all *X Factor* judges. Sharon Osbourne has walked in and out, and Louis Walsh was removed from the line-up and replaced by Brian Friedman, before making a dramatic return early into the filming. Then Cheryl Cole joined the line-up with great success both in terms of popularity, and in terms of her acts. Cole was the winning judge in both of her first two years.

So, as soon as news broke of Dannii's pregnancy, the rumour mill went into overdrive, speculating on how this could affect the 2010 series of *The X Factor*. Some reports suggested that Dannii would leave the show all together, and be replaced by a new judge. Others hinted that she would take a part-time role. Before anything was confirmed, other celebrities began to express their interest in taking part. Having bumped into Simon Cowell in Barbados at Christmas, Sugababes singer Amelle Berrabah was full of praise for him and keen on a part in the show were the chance to arise. 'Simon was amazing. He's such a lovely man – kind and generous and really funny. He has a wicked sense of humour.

We're good mates and obviously he's a great businessman. I'd love to work with him. He's a lot more laid back than you think.' Of a possible space on the *X Factor* panel, she added, 'I'd love the opportunity. It would be brilliant.'

Dannii was clear that it would be – as far as possible – business as usual for her. 'I've got no plans to stop working and take any time off – apart from the actual birth. I've heard I have to be at the birth, right? I'll work it out. I'm not going to start worrying about juggling everything just yet.'

Dannii received plentiful support from other *X Factor* figures when it came to the question of her future on the show. Choreographer (and sometime judge) Brian Friedman said he was concerned that without her the show would lose valuable continuity. 'I'll be really sad if they kick Dannii off the panel,' he said. 'I feel like finally we've got a system and I know how to work with all the judges. It will ruin everything if she goes.'

Even Louis Walsh, who has clashed with Dannii so many times, came out in her support. 'Dannii was so good last year on the show,' he said. 'She was an amazing judge, she worked so hard and she looked fantastic. She's having a baby in July so I don't know if she's coming back to the show or not.' When asked directly whether he expected her to reappear for the new series, Walsh said, 'I hope so.'

With such support coming her way from inside the *X Factor* camp, Dannii's chances of having a significant role in the forthcoming series were definitely increased. Meanwhile, it was reported that an *X Factor* source had said, 'Simon is acutely aware how this could play out in public. He doesn't want to be seen as getting rid of Dannii because she's pregnant but realistically he knows it will be impossible for her to do the whole show from the auditions through to the live finals.'

In April 2010 there were meetings to try to thrash out a way forward, with reports that Dannii would stay on but with a salary that was reduced to reflect her diminished involvement. 'We are very, very keen for her to come back so, at this stage, it doesn't look like her pregnancy is going to present any problems we can't work around,' said a source.

Soon before this the most remarkable Dannii/*X Factor* rumour of them all began to circulate: it was suggested that Kylie might take her place. It seemed unlikely not only because the news broke on 1 April (April Fools' Day) but also because Kylie had previously stated that she would not be able to cope with the challenges of being an *X Factor* judge. Indeed, the ever sharp-tongued Simon Cowell had described Kylie as 'a one-trick pony' in the past. All the same, it took speculation over the issue to new heights prompting a terse but clear denial from Kylie. 'Simon hasn't asked me and probably with good reason. I've said that I'd be really dreadful and my sister is just so great at it and better than I could ever be,' she said.

Dannii – and many of the public – must have wished

that the matter could just be settled once and for all. The endless speculation and hype might have been attractive to the *X Factor* franchise in terms of publicity, but was beginning to become a bore. And there was more to come. Perhaps inevitably the rumour mill tried to use the story of Dannii's pregnancy to hint at a potential reigniting of the 'feud' between her and Cheryl Cole as Cole tried to rebuild her life following the split with her husband Ashley.

Once more, for her part, Dannii felt confident, as it was not uncommon for matters such as this to be settled close to the beginning of filming. 'Last year the contract wasn't signed until June, so she's not worried at all,' said a source. 'She loves *The X Factor* and it is a huge priority for her, so she will do what it takes to make the situation work for everyone.'

Furthermore, she understood that the hype around the show would inevitably largely focus on the judges, the majority of which would be trained on the female judges. 'It's just what fascinates people, I guess,' Dannii said. 'They'd probably struggle to get press coverage on, "Is Louis coming back? And what's he wearing?" '

Meanwhile, she continued to enjoy the challenges of her first pregnancy. 'My boobs are definitely bigger,' she told *Glamour* magazine. 'My tummy's started to change shape, too, although I'm pretty much the same weight. I've not been sick, but I've had moments of feeling nauseous. I've been very, very tired. The first three months were really hard. I'm just coming out of it now,

I hope. There are a lot of changes going on, I can't believe it. We haven't even started thinking of baby names, or whether I'd have the baby at home. The only thing I know is that I'll have the baby in Australia because Kris will be working there. Yay, it'll be an Aussie baby!'

She bonded with fellow celebrity Denise Van Outen, who was expecting her first child with musical star Lee Mead. 'I've been bonding with Dannii over the whole experience – I've given her and Kris a parenting guide called *The Baby Whisperer*,' Van Outen revealed.

Over and over it became clear that Dannii was surrounded by love and support as she prepared for the big day in July 2010.

She may have been spending half her time in Melbourne, but it was good solid British food that she was craving most during her pregnancy. 'I'm craving fish 'n' chips and sticky toffee pudding! Baby "Smithogue" has been enjoying them too much,' she revealed to *OK!* magazine. In time the cravings developed, as she admitted to the same journal. 'I'm eating the most ridiculous amount of cakes but Ferrero Rochers are my favourite,' she said. Meanwhile, she said she was too busy to buy clothes for the baby and hoped that her famous sister would do the styling honours herself. 'I'll be busy doing the mum thing so she can go out and do all the shopping,' said Dannii. 'She's great at all that.' She also predicted that Kylie would be willing to muck in with the babysitting duties, during a chat with the

Metro newspaper. 'Kylie's up for babysitting, I can tell you that much.

'I'll be having an international baby. It's really important to me that the baby knows both places really well. I have lived half my life here now, so the child should see both worlds. Besides, daddy is from here and we both love it here.'

As we have already seen, Kylie had previously predicted that Dannii would be the first of the sisters to become a mum and she was due to be proved correct. However, she confirmed she was keen to follow in her footsteps and become a mother sooner rather than later herself. 'It won't happen just yet but soon I hope, it would be lovely,' she said. 'I've got a new album coming out – I'll have to get that out of the way first.' Dannii revealed that she was very much sharing the joy of her news with her family. 'My brother is thrilled and my sister ... Well, it's a different dynamic between sisters and you just feel like you're sharing that experience, as I'd feel if Kylie had kids first,' she said. 'She loves children, just adores them, so we're sharing it together.'

This sibling sharing of the happiness stood in sharp contrast to a report that had claimed Dannii was terrified about telling Kylie of her pregnancy. The report claimed that for Dannii the prospect of 'breaking the news to her sister was heart-wrenching' due to fears that the revelation would upset her, because Kylie's own chances of conceiving may have been affected by her successful treatment for breast cancer. Dannii firmly denied this story on her official website. And, of course, Kylie had been very upbeat about the news, cheering about it on her Twitter feed.

Even as she prepared for the happiest event of her life to date, Dannii had to deal with renewed sniping from her old *X Factor* adversary Sharon Osbourne. During the publicity rounds to promote her novel, Osbourne reignited the feud with a round of damning verdicts on Dannii and the talent-show genre in general. 'They're queuing up now to get on – what's that show called – We've Got No F**king Talent At All,' she said. 'It's like a revolving door for tw*ts.' Asked about her own previous time as a judge on shows such as *America's Got Talent* and *The X Factor*, Osbourne turned her fire onto Dannii. 'Listen, I actually walked from *X Factor* because I couldn't stand the bullshit any more,' she said of her departure from the show in 2008. 'I was getting well paid – very well paid – so it was hard to leave, but I did because they didn't like me speaking the truth. They'd rather have some doll like Dannii Minogue as judge, endorsing this bullshit. Dannii – I couldn't stand her. She wasn't so much a dim bulb as a bulb in a power cut. F**king useless.'

Harsh words, but sadly this was only the start of the new round of Osbourne abuse. The following day another interview was published in which the rock queen responded to suggestions that Minogue was planning to write about their feud in her forthcoming memoir. In an interview with *Star* magazine, Osbourne seethed, 'She's writing about me now three years after the event! So really I think, Get a life and move on, missus! Move on!' Asked whether she had congratulated Dannii on her pregnancy, the 57-year-old replied, 'Hell, no! I don't like her. I don't like her as a person, I don't like what she represents, and I never will.' Naturally, the press were loving every moment of Osbourne's outspoken tirades and rushed to try to get Dannii to return fire. However, a spokesman told the *Daily Telegraph* that she had no intention of getting involved herself. 'It's all one way from Sharon,' said the spokesman. 'But there's so much good going with Dannii right now that she doesn't worry about it and never has.'

The issue then moved online with Osbourne's daughter Kelly making an impassioned intervention via her Twitter account. 'My mum never said that comment about Dannii,' wrote Osbourne on the social networking site. 'She does not talk about light bulbs and fuses those words are not in my mum's vocabulary!' Kelly continued her statement, reverting at times to capital letters for dramatic emphasis: 'What is wrong with people first I was miss quoted now someone completely made up that's Dannii quote the press can get away with murder! My mum is worse then me she says enough print worthy comments that THEY DONT NEED TO MAKE UP STUPID QUOTES ABOUT DANNII!' She added: 'SHE DID NOT F**KING SAY IT. IT PISSES ME OF MY MUM KEEPS GETTING

DRAGGED INTO THIS BULLS**T I ALMOST FEEL LIKE YOU GUYS WISH SHE HATED DANNII! SHE DOES NOT CARE BUT I DO.' Kelly's statement was not finished yet. She added, 'It 10000000 per cent never came out of my mother's mouth. She is a mother in her 50s (no offense, Mum, you look 30) she is not in HIGH SCHOOL. She works her ass off and does not deserve this! Sorry for getting upset, it's just put the celebrity aside for a second. It's my mother they are talking about! Thank you for your all your support and understanding with my little rant!'

The Twitter website is one used regularly by Dannii and it was there that she made her first public statement on the controversy. 'It is very sad [Osbourne's] anger has now spread to talented hopefuls that enter TV talent competitions,' she wrote. The next words from the Dannii camp came from her boyfriend Kris Smith during an interview in the *Daily Telegraph*. 'I never knew about the animosity between them, so it's all a bit new to me,' he said. With sarcasm, he added, 'But she just seems all class that Sharon, doesn't she? All class, a class act. I have nothing to say to her because I wouldn't fall down that low. It's the way some people are, unfortunately.' During the same interview Smith took the trouble to praise his lady, too. 'Dannii has been absolutely unbelievable and I don't know how she does it with her work schedule while having another life growing inside her – it's mind-boggling and it's amazing,' he said. 'And we're going to have the baby in Melbourne. It's a joint decision and we've talked it over with family over the past few months – things happen so quickly you have to plan ahead. It's best to raise children in Australia because this is the country where the opportunities are.'

Indeed, this was not the only time that Osbourne had returned to the storm. In February 2009, she had appeared on *Piers Morgan's Life Stories*. During a characteristically wide-ranging and frank interview, Morgan naturally pressed his guest to comment on her relationship with Dannii. Osbourne needed little encouragement. She again blamed Dannii for her *X Factor* exit, saying, 'I didn't enjoy working with her at all and the prospect of spending six months sitting next to her, I thought, My life is better than that.' She added that her fellow judge had 'no sense of humour'. Her damning verdict did not stop there and she denied that she had been put out by the arrival of Dannii, a younger co-judge. 'I was 54, been round the block' she said, before adding: 'I've not built my career on my looks or my youth. There was no competition because we're so opposite.'

Osbourne also denied that she hated Dannii, but gave a dismissive reasoning for this. 'I didn't hate her because hatred is very close to love and takes a lot of emotion and I don't have that time for her,' she said. With a final twist of the knife, she added, 'She was like an insect, a mosquito that wouldn't go away.'

And, to be fair, Minogue had been similarly dismissive when Osbourne had originally left *The X Factor*, saying,

'We weren't friends. We weren't always fighting but Sharon made it clear that she didn't like me, so she won't be missed. Not by me.'

Peace of sorts seemed to break out a few weeks later, when Osbourne made some placatory remarks during an interview on radio. Then she went a step further during a chat with *Heat* magazine. She admitted she had not sent Dannii any congratulations on her pregnancy, but added, 'I'm happy for her. I mean, it's the best thing in the world to have a baby. It's the best gift a woman can ever have. It's a blessing, so I'm glad she is.' Of their much-reported rift, she added, 'Not a rift – I just didn't like working with her. There was no competition between us. Not like, "I'm prettier than you, I'm thinner than you, I'm more popular than you." Everybody knows that I'm all of those things! I'm joking! There was never any of that. But as one woman to another, there was no rapport, no respect.' That said, Osbourne had previously given Dannii a backhanded compliment when she said, 'There's the perception [Dannii] is the sweetest little thing in the world but she's not – she's got balls of steel.'

Although the two women would perhaps not like to consider this, they are in many ways cut from the same cloth. Both are fiercely ambitious and both have worked hard to emerge from the shadow of a famous relative – in Osbourne's case her husband Ozzy and in Dannii's case her sister Kylie, of course.

Dannii was down for a gong at the *Elle* Style Awards

in 2010, and she spoke about life as a pregnant mum as she arrived: 'I'm probably doing everything wrong, but I'm enjoying it. I feel good and I've got a gorgeous boyfriend looking after me.' On receiving the TV Star honour at the awards ceremony, she revealed that she was having problems finding clothes to fit her as her pregnancy continued. 'Can't get any of them on and you buy jeans with stretchy bits at the front,' she said, though she was looking stunning in a floor-length yellow gown. 'The rest, I don't even know how it works. I really don't know how I'm going to approach any of it yet.'

She had, though, been signed up to front the advertisement campaign for the new Marks & Spencer clothing range. In these shots Dannii looked healthy and happy, with her arms raised triumphantly in the air in many of them. Alongside her in the M&S adverts were presenter Lisa Snowdon, modelling legend Twiggy, singer VV Brown and model Ana Beatriz Barros. The images were shot in South Africa when Dannii was in the early stages of her pregnancy. She Tweeted details of the shoot to her fans, writing: 'I'm so excited to be a Marks & Spencer girl. On the beach shooting your spring campaign!'

In April 2010, she revealed that – after previously wondering if she would ever record again – she had decided to work on some new musical material. 'I've been keeping it quiet as there is no record deal,' she said. 'But, yeah, I've done a little bit already over the past couple of months. It's all very new. But I have some songs I've co-written and friends have written that ignited my energy to go back to music because I wasn't going to. I was like, "Nah, music is over for me." ' But we'll see. I don't want to put any pressure on myself. I've just run into the studio and done a few hours of work. I still haven't got the demos back yet.'

Among the artists she is thought to have been working with are the Freemasons and Wez Clarke.

Once more, she is not taking this path to compete with Kylie. 'There is honestly no competition between us unless we're on a Scrabble board,' she said, 'then I kick her ass!' She admitted that she did 'look up to' Kylie when as a kid she won a ten-pin bowling contest. Asked what would happen if the two sisters entered *The X Factor* as separate contestants, she laughed and said, 'I think she'd kick my ass!'

However, a more significant fashion deal was struck by her at this point. She signed a deal with Australian department store chain David Jones to sell her new collection – Project D. It was quickly noted that this deal put her in a rival position to her partner Kris, who is with the Myer menswear firm. Not that such professional issues would stop her supporting him for a moment, and, as a Myer spokesperson said, there would be no issues about the deal from their end. 'Dannii is always welcome to attend a Myer shop and we hope that she is able to attend to watch Kris,' he said, ahead of a fashion show in 2010.

As if the proud and supportive Dannii could ever have been kept away, anyway!

All the same, she obviously has high hopes for the Project D range. This was shown when she boasted that she had designed a dress specifically with America's first lady Michelle Obama in mind. 'I have a Project D dress for Michelle!' She had created the range with a friend called Tabitha and was determined to make it work. 'This is my first leap into the UK fashion scene and I am putting everything on the line to make this something beautiful that women love,' said Dannii.

There are plans to make a television series that would follow the creation and subsequent fortunes of the range. And, as always, Dannii's aspirations cross several fronts. She has flown to America to discuss acting roles and has reportedly auditioned for parts in hit dramas *Desperate Housewives* and *Ugly Betty*.

As she prepared for a new addition to the family, Dannii was also mourning the loss of another. Her great-uncle Dennis Riddiford died in February aged 80. The retired carpenter was the brother of their grandmother Millie Jones, who moved to Queensland in 1955. He had been following his great-nieces' fortunes right into old age and had even spoken publicly when Kylie fought breast cancer. 'She's done marvellous – just fantastic,' he said proudly of her.

She continued her judging duties on *Australia's Got Talent* in March and April 2010, deep into her pregnancy. Ever the professional, she turned up to work each day and looked absolutely stunning as she wore a black one-shoulder dress, with a multicoloured scarf tied over her opposite shoulder. These were happy times for the heavily pregnant Dannii, who shared her joy with her Twitter followers. 'It is gorgeous and sunny in Perth today. Off to auditions, so bring it on Perth!'

Indeed, as she told Australia's *Who* magazine, she was feeling increasingly comfortable in her own skin as a result of falling pregnant. 'Since I've been pregnant now, I'm just, like, "Aah!" It's an acceptance of your body; it's been really good. I thought it was absolutely going to freak me out, the whole body change and hormonal change. But I am loving it.' And even before her first baby was born, Dannii was already hinting that she and Kris had discussed having more in the near future. 'Maybe we'll have a brood of kids,' she said. But Dannii is not naïve about the challenges that parenthood will bring to her life. When speaking about her relationship with her parents, she speaks warmly, but honestly. Admitting that they have clashed at times, she asked rhetorically: 'You know, what are children for except to make your life hell?'

When Kris posted a photograph of a Babygro they had purchased for their forthcoming baby, there was speculation that the couple must have been expecting a boy, as the garment was a very boyish style. 'Our first baby purchase,' wrote Kris on Twitter as he posted the photograph. When fans asked whether this meant they were expecting a boy, he did not reply. And Dannii had already confirmed that she was not expecting twins – 'I wouldn't be able to stand up,' she laughed.

But, regardless of the child's gender, these are happy times for Dannii as she comfortably moves into her more mature years. 'I feel as though a whole life chapter is closing, and a new exciting one is unfolding,' she said in 2010. Far from fearing growing older, Dannii now seems to be relishing every new moment. 'Nobody ever tells you about all the good stuff involved in getting older. You're no longer in such a rush and you're more confident. I feel more relaxed now than ever. Seriously, if a genie gave me the chance to go back in time, I'd tell him I was only interested in moving forward.'

Throughout her life, Dannii has been an inspiration to many of her fans, and the glamorous way in which she is embracing her advancing years is just another fine example that many will aim to emulate.

Might marriage be on the cards for her and Kris? She admits she was 'destroyed' for a while by her split with McMahon. 'I am really frightened by marriage now,' she said in the wake of the split. 'I won't say never again, but it does scare me. My visions of marriage are so different to when I was totally naïve and wide-eyed and got married ages ago. Also, times have changed. Marriages seem less important and relationships are like phases. Don't get me wrong, relationships are still deep and important, but the concept of being with someone for ever may be extinct. My parents are still together, still in love and that's a rare thing.'

However, much water has travelled under the bridge since then, so do not be surprised if Dannii does walk down the aisle again soon.

Speculation naturally mounts about where she, Kris and their first child – boy or girl – will ultimately settle. Perhaps the real answer is that they will always be rather mobile, though London does hold a special charm for Dannii. Having arrived nervously in the UK all those years ago, she now feels extremely happy here. 'It's all very comfortable and I feel really welcome here, but it's not a place I would choose to live in: I'm here for work,' she has said. 'I'm not really a city person. I like nature, water, the outdoors and good weather – all the things I grew up with, and that's not London. My long-term objective is to live in the South of France, work in London and spend at least a month a year in Australia.' Talk about living the dream!

Career-wise she is, she says, loath to plan ahead. Although to outsiders Dannii seems to be a determined careerist, she says that she actually cherishes the freedom of not constantly looking ahead. 'If you ask me how I've steered my career, I'll tell you that I haven't,' she said. 'I hate planning. I never know what I'm doing in 12 months, let alone when people say, "Where do you see yourself in five years' time?" If I knew where I want to be in five years' time, just put me in an old people's home right now,' she says, laughing. 'I love not knowing – knowing your job is secure and safe, knowing what's around the corner. I think I'd really freak out if I had job security.'

That said, reports in April 2010 suggested that Dannii had the security of another *X Factor* series after a successful lunch with producer Richard Holloway. She was reported to have been offered £700,000 this time, to reflect what would be a reduced role, due to her pregnancy.

Nobody should expect Dannii to step away from the public eye – nor will she stop being forthright any time soon. She has always been and will probably always be a straight-talker. 'I probably go that little bit too far, but that's the extent of my personality,' she admitted. 'I'm strong, not wishy-washy. I want to say, This is it. Do you like it or do you hate it?'

When it comes to that question over Dannii, the world increasingly likes it. Even as she remains a frank and open person, she has become a little more mellow as the years pass. 'I used to get very stressed about everything, but I think now I'm older, I'm learning to be more easygoing,' she said.

That notwithstanding, Dannii is a survivor and a fighter. Her determination, ambition and enormous stamina have seen her a fixture in the world of entertainment for over 30 years. You don't last that long without having something very special about you. Kylie might be queen of the world in the eyes of many, but for Dannii's fans she will always be so much more than a princess. She has found true love as she approaches her forties and has also become more loved than ever by the public. She says she would have happily settled for just the first of these developments, 'but to have both happen at once has been just incredible'.

Long may she reign, but, when she finally looks back over her whole eventful life, what would be her chosen epitaph? 'She took it one day at a time,' said Dannii. It would be a modest but strangely fitting epitaph for this inspiring woman's life.

bibliography

Alexandra Burke: A Star is Born, Chas Newkey-Burden, John Blake 2009

Kylie: The Biography, Sean Smith, Pocket Books 2006

Kylie: Queen of the World, Julie Aspinall, John Blake 2008

Simon Cowell: The Unauthorised Biography, Chas Newkey-Burden, Michael O'Mara 2009

The X Factor Companion, Jordan Paramour, Headline 2007

Acknowledgements

Thanks to John Blake, Lucian Randall, Chris Morris, Luke Bayer and Maurice Maurice.